an illustrated intr

THE FIRST WORLD

Phil Carradice

First published 2014

Amberley Publishing
The Hill, Stroud
Gloucestershire, GL5 4EP

www.amberley-books.com

British Library Cataloguing in Publication Data.
A catalogue record for this book is available from the British Library.

ISBN 978 1 4456 3296 4 (paperback)
ISBN 978 1 4456 3305 3 (ebook)

Typesetting and Origination by Amberley Publishing.
Printed in Great Britain.

CONTENTS

NORWAY
CHRISTIANAN
STAVANAG
NORTH SEA
ABERDEN
PERTH
EDINBURGH
GLASGAW
Newcastle
Hull
Leeds
LONDON
PORTSMOUTH
Havre
Reval
Riga
Lebau
Kown
GERMAN NAVY
BERLIN
DENZIG
GERMAN ARMY
POLAND
WARSAW
Lubin
Cracaw
Lemberg
ANTWERP
PARIS
ORLEANS
Belfort
Dijon
BERNE
SWITZ
FRANCE
Lyons
Marseilles
MILAN
TRIEST
GENOA
AUSTRIA-HUNGARY
Bukarest
BELGRADE
SERVIA
Montenegro
ADRIATIC SEA
FLORENCE
ROME
CORSICA
SARDINIA
Naples
BRINDISI
ALBANIA
Palermo
SICILY
Messina
MALTA
To Egypt
Tunis
Algieres
AFRICA
Majorca

THE FIRST WORLD WAR
IN FIVE MINUTES

The First World War erupted in August 1914, the first global conflict in the history of mankind. It was a war that was fought right across the northern and southern hemispheres and had ramifications on all of the world's great continents.

It was a war that involved many nations, large and small, a war that, over a period of four years, caused millions of casualties. It saw the end of dynasties that had ruled in Europe for thousands of years and brought new countries, squealing and kicking, into the world. It bankrupted the nations of Europe and allowed the USA to assume an all-powerful economic position that it has never lost or relinquished. It was a truly seminal event, one that has shaped our understanding of modern times.

The causes of the war were numerous but, in many respects, it came about when the game of brinkmanship that had been played for years by the great states of Europe, Germany, France, Russia, Austria-Hungary and Britain, reached a point where the bluff was finally called and nobody was prepared to back down.

Suspicion and obligation played an inevitable part, every nation afraid that its rivals would form alliances that would leave them isolated and vulnerable. With no mechanism then in existence to arbitrate in any case of international dispute, alliances between the nations were formed, alliances that created opposing power blocks and eventually dragged everyone into the war.

The match that sparked the conflict was the assassination of Archduke Franz Ferdinand, heir to the Austrian throne, by a Serbian nationalist at Sarajevo on 28 June 1914. Starting with Austria playing the heavy hand against Serbia, over the summer months of 1914 ultimatums were given and ignored, one side after the other falling into the trap of declaring war in support of their allies. The armed

Opposite page: The Kaiser, autocratic ruler of Germany, had long been seen as a threat to the peace of Europe – as this political cartoon from the early months of the First World War clearly shows.

camps that had been created by the complicated series of alliances saw Germany and Austria-Hungary lining up against France and Russia.

Britain, supposedly honouring an ancient treaty to defend the sovereignty of Belgium but in reality protecting its position of power in Europe, declared war on Germany on 4 August. As the war ground on, other countries, like Italy, Turkey and Bulgaria, also joined in the conflict.

Within days, huge armies were marching across Europe. German forces stormed through Belgium, destroying the frontier fortresses and threatening Paris as French and British armies fell back before the onslaught. The Schlieffen Plan, a lightning-fast right hook through Belgium and northern France, designed by the German Chief of Staff many years before, was essential if Germany was to knock France out of the war before the Russian juggernaut began to roll in the east; a war on two fronts was to be avoided at all costs.

In the end that is exactly what they got. The German Army advanced so quickly that it outran its lines of supply and support. Soldiers were exhausted by the speed of the attacks and the advance was halted at the Battle of the Marne. Neither side had any alternative but to establish defensive lines, which soon stretched 400 miles across Europe from the coast of Belgium to the border of Switzerland. With minor alterations, this line of trenches, fortresses and dugouts remained in almost exactly the same position for the next four years.

The war ably demonstrated the power of defensive as opposed to offensive combat, as weapons such as heavy machine guns, gas and artillery consistently destroyed all attempts to breach the opposition lines. Barbed wire and the bloody killing ground of no man's land were the symbols of the war, but artillery shells and machine-gun fire kept both sides pinned down in a morass of mud, blood and grinding slaughter.

None of this prevented the two sides mounting hugely expensive assaults each year. The battles of Ypres and Loos resulted in enormous casualty figures. Neither of them came close to the carnage of the Battle of the Somme in 1916, when both Germany and Britain lost half a million men. On the opening day alone Britain suffered 20,000 casualties, the largest and most appalling death toll the British Army has ever endured on a single day.

The war might have been centred on what soon became known as the Western Front, but there were other theatres of war where the campaigning was just as significant.

In 1915, the Dardanelles Campaign saw British, Colonial and French troops landed on the Gallipoli Peninsula of Turkey in what could and should have been a deadly blow to the soft underbelly of the Axis forces. As it turned out, it was a costly and ill-managed affair where half of the Allied casualties came from fever as opposed to battle wounds. The campaign was eventually abandoned in January 1916, but not before its architect, Winston Churchill, First Lord of the Admiralty, had been forced from office.

Fighting took place in the Holy Land in a campaign that saw the emergence of the mercurial Lawrence of Arabia. Britain needed the Arab people to fight with her and Lawrence undoubtedly fostered their belief that support for Britain now would lead to independence and the creation of an Arab homeland once the war was won. It was not to be.

Britain had the most powerful navy in the world and, after initial setbacks like the Battle of Coronel, where the German Admiral Maximilian von Spee emerged triumphant, the Royal Navy soon re-established itself as the premier maritime nation.

The only time that the battle fleets of Britain and Germany, major contributors to the tension between the two countries in the run-up to the war, came to blows was at the Battle of Jutland. It was a marginal tactical victory for Germany but a huge strategic one for Britain, as the German High Seas Fleet never left port again, except to surrender in November 1918.

The First World War saw the development of a vast range of new weapons. Tanks, submarines and aircraft came into their own as weapons of war and gas was used in combat for the first time. America, initially content to remain on the sidelines, making vast profits in the process, finally joined the Allies in 1917. It was a timely intervention as the Czar of Russia had fallen from power after the Bolshevik Revolution and Russia had, by the end of the year, sued for peace.

The slaughter went on for four years, the last German attacks of 1918 exhausting what little stamina and raw materials the country had left. With American troops pouring into Europe in ever-increasing numbers, the Allies began to push back the German forces until, in November 1918, Kaiser Wilhelm II, the German Emperor, abdicated and the German government was forced to ask for an armistice. At 11.00 a.m. on 11 November 1918, the guns finally stopped.

Nearly 10 million men had died in the war, many more being injured and maimed. They were shot, blown up and drowned in mud and water as the warring powers found increasingly efficient but barbaric ways of killing their opponents.

The war to end all wars, as it was originally billed, was nothing of the sort, and twenty-one years later it all began again, this time on an even larger and more dramatic scale. That is surely the ultimate tragedy of the First World War.

TIMELINE

- **4 August 1914**

  Britain declares war when Germany ignores the British ultimatum to pull her troops out of Belgium and within days the British Expeditionary Force, under the command of Sir John French, leaves for France.

- **September 1914**

  The German advance is halted by the French under General Joseph 'Papa' Joffre at the Battle of the Marne. German forces retreat to the line of the River Aisne. Here both sides dig in, creating the line of trenches that survives virtually intact until 1918.

  In the east, German forces under von Hindenburg and Ludendorff defeat the invading Russian armies at the Battle of Tannenberg. Some 90,000 Russians become prisoners.

- **1 November 1914**

  A weak British squadron under Admiral Craddock is annihilated at the Battle of Coronel, the first British naval defeat for over 100 years. Revenge comes a few weeks later when Admiral Sturdee defeats the German Admiral von Spee at the Battle of the Falkland Islands.

  The Dardanelles/Gallipoli Campaign begins in 1915 when British and Anzac troops (New Zealand and Australian) go ashore on the Gallipoli Peninsula. It is a muddled campaign that sees no progress and the troops are evacuated at the end of the year.

- **September 1915**

  The Battle of Loos. British losses of 43,000.

- **21 February 1916**

  The Battle of Verdun begins, a slogging match that lasts for months and causes 400,000 French and 350,000 German casualties.

- **31 May 1916**

  The Battle of Jutland takes place. The British lose more ships but the German High Seas Fleet retreats to port, where it remains for the next two years.

1 July 1916

Partly in an attempt to ease pressure on the French, Sir Douglas Haig launches the Battle of the Somme, the huge British volunteer army going into action for the first time. By the time the battle peters out in November both sides have lost half a million men.

7 December 1916

David Lloyd George becomes Prime Minister of Britain.

March 1917

The Russian Revolution breaks out. Czar Nicholas is taken prisoner by the revolutionaries but, for the moment, Russia continues to fight on.

April 1917

The USA declares war on Germany; from now on, the defeat of Germany is only a matter of time.

In the wake of disastrous losses in the so-called Nivelle Offensive, the French Army mutinies. For several weeks the way to Paris is wide open but the Germans simply do not realise.

31 July 1917

The Third Battle of Ypres (Passchendaele as it is known) begins. The battle is fought in thick mud and horrendous rain.

November 1917

The November Revolution in Russia brings the Bolsheviks under Lenin to power and effectively removes Russia from the war.

General Allenby, greatly helped by the guerrilla war of T. E. Lawrence, begins to make definite progress in the war in the Middle East.

February 1918

The German U-boat campaign proves so successful that food rationing is introduced in Britain.

21 March 1918

The Ludendorff Offensive is launched. It is a last-gasp attempt to wrest victory from the Allies before the American troops arrive in great numbers.

8 August 1918

The Allies counter-attack. German troops have been so demoralised and worn out by their own offensives that they fall back all the way along the line.

October 1918

With starvation and revolution becoming real possibilities, Germany asks for peace. The Kaiser abdicates, and on 11 November 1918 an armistice is signed in a railway carriage in the forest of Compiègne. The war is over.

YOUR COUNTRY'S CALL

Isn't this worth fighting for?
ENLIST NOW

1
THE CATALYST

For the British, the First World War began on 4 August 1914. Its causes are many and varied and while a killing in Sarajevo may have been the match that blew the powder keg, the fuse had been simmering for many years.

Germany had not existed before 1870, when Otto von Bismarck forged a united Germany out of several disparate states. Victory in the Franco–Prussian War of 1870 merely confirmed the strength of this dynamic nation in the heart of Europe.

However, industrialists in Germany soon decided that they did not need war with any of the other great nations. Economic strength alone would soon elevate the country to the forefront of European powers.

Military minds thought differently and by 1914 the German Army had become the most powerful fighting force in the world. Knowing that the key to the country's economic and colonial success was her navy, Germany was also engaged in an arms race with Britain, building dreadnought battleships at a phenomenal rate.

Yet things were not quite as clear-cut as they seemed. The armies of France and Russia were also growing and within a few years they would undoubtedly match the strength of Germany. For every dreadnought built by Germany, Britain – unwilling to relinquish her position as the world's premier trading nation – was building two more.

Arguably, then, August 1914 was the ideal moment for Germany to start a war, before it was too late. And yet, in that last glorious summer, it seemed as if the great powers were closer in understanding and viewpoint than they had ever been.

Kaiser Wilhelm, George V and Czar Nicholas were cousins who, almost to the end, maintained friendly relations with each other. And, on the surface at least, it appeared that the French were moving to a position of tentative friendship with Germany. Yet again it paid to look deeper as this was a veneer that covered too many cracks.

All of the great powers were naturally suspicious of each other, afraid that alliances would be formed between enemies or rivals, leaving them alone and isolated. There was no mechanism in existence at that time to settle or arbitrate in disputes and in many quarters war was regarded as a natural consequence that might renew and refresh a nation's blood stock.

Seeing no other way, in the early years of the twentieth century the great powers began to form alliances with each other, alliances that, once war began, would start to tumble like a stack of dominoes.

Germany and Austria–Hungary, always natural allies, soon signed a mutual defence pact. In 1901 France and Russia did likewise, the Czar promising that in the event of war between Germany and France, Russia would launch an attack on Germany within eighteen days. Britain, protected by the Royal Navy, maintained an aloof stance, although she did reach a diplomatic understanding with France, her traditional enemy. In 1907 she came to a similar arrangement with Russia, thus creating the Entente Cordiale.

These alliances seemed to determine the safety of each individual country and guarantee the peace of Europe. In reality they were rigid stockades that did little more than ensure that if one great power went to war with another, the rest of Europe would be quickly dragged in.

ASSASSINATION

The immediate cause of war was the assassination of Archduke Franz Ferdinand, heir to the twin thrones of Austria and Hungary, on 28 June 1914.

Bosnia and Herzegovina had been annexed by Austria–Hungary in 1908. These Balkan provinces contained over 20 million Serbs, Slavs and Croats and with Serbia increasingly seeing herself as the leader of a Pan-Slav movement, there was resentment, particularly among the young, that they had become part of the Hapsburg Empire.

Students gathered together in cities like Sarajevo to plan how they might change things. Wanting independence from foreign rule was nothing new – what was different was the willingness of these students to use violence to achieve their aims. So when it was announced that Archduke Franz Ferdinand, heir to the Hapsburg monarchy, would come to inspect the Austrian Army outside Sarajevo in the early summer of 1914, a group of young Serbs decided they would try to assassinate him.

The students were given weapons by a Serbian secret society called the Black Hand. The links between the Black Hand and the Serbian government remain unclear but over the next few weeks the students carefully laid their plans.

Franz Ferdinand and his wife Sophie arrived in Sarajevo on the morning of 28

The Archduke Franz Ferdinand, heir to the Austro-Hungarian throne, and his wife Sophie are seen here on a state occasion. As she was not of the same rank as him (theirs was a morganatic marriage) they were only occasionally seen together in public and moments like this were unusual.

June. At first, however, things did not go quite the way the students had planned.

One of them lost his nerve and returned home before the archduke even appeared. Another hurled a bomb at the royal car as it passed. The bomb hit the hood, bounced into the road and exploded in front of the car behind. Several of the conspirators, hearing the explosion, either ran for cover or failed to intervene and the archduke's car drove on to a reception at the town hall.

Due to the assassination attempt, the route of the archduke's return journey was now changed to take the fast way out of town, down the long, straight road known as Appel Quay. Unfortunately, nobody thought of telling the drivers.

The leading car slowed and turned into Franz Joseph Street. The archduke's vehicle began to follow. Then, realising the mistake, the drivers stopped their cars and prepared to reverse. But the error had brought Franz Ferdinand under the gun of Gavrilo Princip, the most dedicated of all the would-be assassins.

Princip took aim and fired twice. At first it seemed as if the shots had missed their mark but as the car began to move once more the duchess fell across the lap of her husband. And then aides saw blood begin to spurt from Franz Ferdinand's mouth.

The archduke collapsed, muttering, 'It's nothing, nothing.' Glancing down at his wife, he whispered, 'Sophie, live for the children.' The car was driven rapidly to a nearby hospital but it was no use. Franz Ferdinand had been hit by a single shot, the bullet lodging in his spine, and he breathed his last shortly after reaching the hospital. Sophie had died a few minutes earlier.

2

1914: THE GUNS OF AUGUST

MOBILISATION

The Austro–Hungarian government was adamant that they knew where the blame lay for the assassination of Franz Ferdinand. Backed by their German allies, they decided it was time to take a hard line with Serbia and on 25 July 1914 the Serbs were presented with an ultimatum.

The ultimatum was designed to humiliate, requiring Serbia, among other things, to suppress all anti-Austrian societies and remove from the army anyone who was suspected of anti-Austrian sympathies. Nobody expected Serbia to accept the terms but, desperate to avoid further bloodshed, the Serbian government agreed to eight out of the ten demands. The two that had been rejected were so minor that nobody even considered them worth bothering with.

The mood in Vienna, however, was belligerent. The heir to the Hapsburg monarchy had been killed and many Austrians felt that something had to be done to put the Serbs in their place. The reply was not good enough and three days later Austria–Hungary declared war on Serbia.

Russia, as a predominantly Slav state, had long felt under an obligation to support Serbia in any conflict – and, of course, German/Austrian dominance in the Balkans, blocking and controlling the way to Constantinople, could not be tolerated. On 30 July 1914 Russia mobilised her forces. The Russians did not want war – this was merely a game of brinkmanship, an answer to Austria–Hungary's aggressive posturing.

Russia had a huge standing army, over 1 million men, plus a vast reserve of conscript soldiers. To mobilise these forces was a major undertaking that relied heavily on the Russian railway system. Once the railway trains and wagons began to roll they had to continue moving, otherwise there would be an enormous log jam of men and machinery.

Mobilisation was a dilemma that also faced Germany. If the Germans did not immediately mobilise against Russia, they would soon be fighting a war on two

Political cartoonists were quick to make capital out of the threats and posturing of the Kaiser, Kaiser Bill as he was dubbed. This unusual postcard from the first year of the war shows the Kaiser and his ally, Austria, facing the might of the Allies – on a golf course!

fronts as France, already joined by treaty to Russia, had indicated that she would abide by the terms of their agreement.

As a consequence, Germany sent an ultimatum to Russia, demanding that she demobilise her forces. It was refused and, on 1 August, Germany declared war on Russia. Two days later, in an attempt to pre-empt the French, war was also declared on France. Almost without realising it, the great powers of Europe had slid into a war.

For a while Britain remained on the sidelines. Germany had been only too aware that she might, one day, have to fight a war on two fronts, against Russia and France at the same time. Count von Schlieffen, Chief of the German General Staff between 1891 and 1907, had come up with an ingenious plan of campaign. The frontier between Germany and France was short and heavily defended but to the north lay the relatively open plains of Belgium.

Although a neutral country, a lightning strike through Belgium, followed by an encircling right hook to the south and east, should knock France out of the war in six weeks. It was a desperate plan but, in light of the alliances and power blocks between the nations, it was the only one that Germany possessed.

Von Schlieffen had been dead for almost half a dozen years when, on 2 August, Germany demanded free passage for her armies through Belgium. The Belgians refused and when German troops rolled, regardless, into the country on 4 August, Britain found herself on the edge of conflict.

In a treaty signed seventy-four years earlier, Britain had guaranteed Belgium's territorial safety, a treaty so ancient that many people thought it had lapsed. It hadn't, and Britain had little alternative but to stand by her obligations. A British ultimatum for German forces to leave Belgian territory expired, unanswered, at midnight on 4 August, and almost before people knew what was happening Britain found herself at war with Germany.

BRITAIN AT WAR

4 August 1914 was a bank holiday in Britain, a day of stupendous heat. When people returned from their excursions to Brighton or Southend later that night they learned that the country was about to go to war with Germany. The news was greeted not with shock or horror but an outpouring of excitement.

Crowds thronged the Mall, singing and screaming for the king to show himself on the balcony of Buckingham Palace. The Kaiser, the man who had dared to challenge the might of the Royal Navy, was at last about to receive a 'bloody nose'. But for those in the know, for those with a deeper understanding of the ramifications of war, there were many reservations.

That night Sir Edward Grey, British Foreign Secretary, apparently stood at his window and watched a lamplighter at work in the street outside. 'The lights are going out all over Europe,' he supposedly remarked. 'I do not think we shall see them lit again in our time.' Whether or not Grey actually uttered those words is a matter of conjecture but they certainly caught the mood of the moment.

Reservists were called up, along with Territorials, part-time soldiers who, initially at least, were intended to serve only in Britain. The last conflict between the major European powers had been the Franco–Prussian War of 1870 and Britain had not been involved. Nobody in 1914 had the slightest idea of what was waiting for them.

Britain had always depended on the Royal Navy for defence and the British Army stood at just 250,000 men – a mere handful when compared to the 800,000 of Germany and the million plus available to Russia – used simply to take part in the odd colonial skirmish. In August 1914 many of these troops were still serving in distant parts of the Empire. It would be months before they could be recalled. However, treaty obligations meant that Britain was now committed to sending an expeditionary force to fight in France and Belgium. In the days ahead Britain would require a volunteer army of some size and substance.

Right: Surely the most famous recruiting poster of all time. Lord Kitchener glares at passers-by and dares them to rcfusc thc call to arms. Kitchener asked for – and got – 100,000 volunteers and more to shore up the ranks of the British Army.

Below: Thousands quickly answered the call to 'join up'. This photograph from August 1914 shows rows of men in London, all waiting to enlist – it was a scene that was replicated in every other city in the country.

The British Expeditionary Force was quickly assembled, 90,000 men in one cavalry and four infantry divisions. Under the command of Sir John French, by 8 August they were beginning to take ship for France. They came ashore, in the main, at Le Havre and moved to a concentration area by train and, in some cases, by London busses that had been hastily pressed into service. By 13 August they had taken up position on the left flank of the French Army and had begun to move forward into Belgium.

THE FIRST SHOTS

Adhering to the Schlieffen Plan, the German High Command also acted swiftly. Between 4 and 6 August over 500 railway trains thundered across the Rhine bridges as German forces under generals von Kluck and von Bulow poured like marauding ants into Belgium.

The border towns of Namur and Liege were battered by heavy artillery shells and the Belgians pulled back to Antwerp, destroying railway lines and rolling stock behind them as they went. This scorched earth policy caused major disruption to the German Army, slowing but not stopping the advance.

Inevitably, there were tales of atrocities committed by the 'barbaric' German invaders, stories that were embellished many times. Atrocities did take place and the Germans were undoubtedly harsh in their treatment of some villages and towns. But the stories of burning babies and the massacre of nuns that were commonplace in the British press were gross exaggerations with one purpose – to put the whole of Britain behind the war effort.

Meanwhile the French, under Joseph 'Pappa' Joffre, decided that attack was the best form of defence and, in the wooded Ardennes region, the French Army cut into the wheeling left flank of the encircling Germans. Clad in their traditional blue-and-red uniforms, the French were mown down in their thousands. In support, the British Expeditionary Force advanced steadily towards the Sambre River and the line of the Mons–Conde Canal.

The first contact between British and German forces came at Mons on 23 August when two British divisions were attacked by considerably larger German forces. So accurate was the British rifle fire – supposedly fifteen rounds rapid in a minute – that the Germans thought they were being fired on by machine guns. In the face of such a fusillade, the German advance ground to a halt.

The legend of the Angel of Mons dates from this time, the legend stating that British troops were aided by phantom archers and an angel during the battle

The last stand of L Battery of the Royal Horse Artillery during the first contact between British and German forces, the Battle of Mons in August 1914. In a short and sharp engagement, L Battery was virtually wiped out but eight German guns were also destroyed.

– a story that owes far more to the imaginative pen of Welsh journalist Arthur Machen than it does to reality. Another popular story from these weeks was of Russian soldiers seen marching through France or Scotland – the location varies – with snow on their boots. In reality these 'Russians' were probably members of a Scottish Regiment, wearing white spats and talking in a broad Highland brogue that would have been unintelligible to most people.

Following the clash at Mons, Sir John French had intended to fight again the following day. Then he was informed that the French were withdrawing, moving back to defend Paris. Realising that the BEF (British Expeditionary Force) was now totally isolated, Sir John had no option but to order a similar withdrawal, a hard-fighting retreat through boiling heat, pursued by a dogged and determined enemy. Several times the BEF was in danger of being completely cut off, only last-ditch stands by individual units of infantry and artillery saving the day.

On 26 August Sir John French decided to turn and fight once more. At the Battle of Le Cateau the Germans were halted yet again. It was a brutal and hard-fought slugging match but it gave the British – and their exhausted enemy – a breathing space of almost ten days.

Above left: The legend of the Angel of Mons, along with another fanciful story of phantom British bowmen helping Allied troops, was used to bolster British morale.

Above right: Lord Kitchener was appointed Secretary of State for War on 6 August. Despite his clear limitations as a military strategist, Kitchener was alone in thinking the war would last for several years.

SELLING THE WAR

It was a time for heroes. As early as 6 August, Field Marshal Kitchener, the victor of the Sudan, had been appointed Secretary of State for War. With everyone predicting that the war would be over by Christmas – even the Kaiser commented that his troops would be back in Germany 'before the leaves fall from the trees' – Kitchener shocked the establishment by declaring that it would last for at least three years.

Kitchener proposed that an army of 100,000 volunteers should be immediately raised. And to help in creating this new volunteer army, recruiting posters, backed up by recruiting events, were in evidence all over the country. Lord Kitchener's face seemed to stare out from every hoarding and men flocked to the colours in their thousands. They were not soldiers, however, and training them for the task would take time.

Kitchener's target, the first 100,000 men, was easily reached and then superseded many times. It seemed as if every able-bodied man in the country was either in the Army or about to join up. In an age when geographical mobility was unheard of, when men lived and died in the town or village where they had been born, it was an adventure to join the Army, to sail off to foreign climes with friends from the factory or farmyard.

Even so, there were those who did not want to go. This was the time of 'the white feather', a token of cowardice that was presented to any man not in uniform or suspected of malingering, while papers like *The Penarth Times* in South Wales were more than happy to lend weight to the recruiting campaign:

> Our young men go about in their tennis rig-outs or parade on the Esplanade, smirking at girls. Is it fair that they should go about so callously while those who took up arms with our promised support, lie cold and stiff. Give the laggards their marching orders, shame them into understanding where their duty lies.

There were many complex and diverse reasons for Britain joining in what was, essentially, a European conflict but the German attack through Belgium was a great excuse. Propagandists and recruiting agencies shamelessly exploited the idea of 'gallant little Belgium' with a call to avenge the wrong done to her by a brutal and ambitious Germany.

PAINTING

As early as August 1914 the British government realised that the country was lagging far behind Germany as far as propaganda was concerned. As a result, the British War Propaganda Bureau was formed under Charles Masterman.

When the bureau published a report into the German atrocities in Belgium they illustrated it with the work of Dutch artist Louis Raemaekers. His graphic depictions of the 'rapacious Hun' brought a stunning response from the public, and Masterman realised the value of art as a propaganda tool. He decided to send professional artists out to France to depict life in the trenches.

Muirhead Bone was the first official war artist but over the next few years he was joined by over ninety fellow artists. Many of their paintings were so realistic that they were only able to be shown after the war. Restrictions did relax once Lord Beaverbrook took over as Minister for Information in 1918, but the conflict between reality and propaganda remained in place until the end.

THE BATTLE OF THE MARNE

After a ten-day respite, the German juggernaut began to roll again. Now, von Kluck's First Army swung to the left, eastwards of Paris where he felt there were better lines of communication with the forces of his compatriot Prince von Bulow.

This drastic change of direction utterly destroyed von Schlieffen's carefully worked-out strategy but by 5 September German troops had crossed the River Marne. Here they were immediately harried by the armies of Gallieni, the military governor of Paris, and by those of 'Pappa' Joffre. Despite desperate French attacks, the Germans moved onwards, some units of their army eventually finding themselves within 15 miles of the French capital.

On 7 September General Gallieni created one of the great legends of the war when he ordered every taxicab in Paris to be commandeered by the military. Filled with replacements and reserves, these taxis then took the soldiers 40 miles to the front, several of them making five or six journeys each.

Faced by furious assaults from Gallieni on his flank, von Kluck withdrew his leading troops in order to deal with these French attacks. It opened a 30-mile-wide gap between the two German armies, and into this, Joffre insisted that John French must thrust the BEF. To the amazement of Sir John he found virtually no opposition even though his allies were fighting desperately on either side of him.

At this crucial moment, as in so much of the war, British leadership promptly failed. Sir John French seemed incapable of using his initiative. His advance was too slow and failed to exploit the gap, even though, on occasions, his leading cavalry detachments were 20 or 30 miles behind the German front line.

Despite this clear failure in leadership, the appearance of British troops was disheartening for the Germans and von Moltke felt he had no alternative but to order a withdrawal. Soon the tactical withdrawal became a full-scale retreat. It was a distressing moment for the German troops – they had, after all, been within touching distance of their objective.

THE RACE TO THE SEA

The German retreat lasted for just over five days. They fell back on all flanks, searching for the most suitable spot to stabilise their line. They found it along the River Aisne where they were at last able to set up defensive positions.

Both sides 'dug in', creating trenches to protect themselves and to mount what was already becoming one of the most significant weapons of the war, the machine gun. Sir John French, proving himself a more effective prophet than general, remarked, 'I think the battle of the Aisne is very typical of what battles in the future are most likely to resemble – the spade will be as great a necessity as the rifle.'

As it stood, the flanks of both the Germans and the Allies remained wide open, particularly in the north, between the Aisne and the sea. In a desperate attempt to get around, or turn the others' flank, there now began what is known as the 'race to the sea'.

The BEF swept towards St Omer and Ypres. Both towns were strategically significant, St Omer blocking the way to Boulogne, Ypres the way to Calais. The Channel ports were important for the British as places that, should they be needed, could act as bases for evacuation.

At Ypres the British line bulged out into German territory, creating a salient that as the war progressed would become the site of the greatest prolonged bloodbath Europe had ever seen.

The First Battle of Ypres took place in October 1914, during the race to the sea. The Germans advanced on Ypres at exactly the same moment as the British came up from the south and the two forces ran into each other.

When the Battle of Ypres petered out, the salient remained in British hands. British casualties numbered some 50,000, a mere handful when compared to the German losses of 150,000, but these were the cream of British soldiery, the backbone of the small but highly professional British Army. These 'Old Contemptibles' were the men who, for years, had served throughout the Empire. They had fought, bravely and magnificently, at Mons and Le Cateau. Now, largely, they were gone.

In the future their places would be taken by the vast volunteer armies that were beginning to build back home in Britain. But it would take time for these replacements to arrive, let alone become an effective fighting force. For the time being the French would have to shoulder the burden.

Britain and France had been traditional enemies for hundreds of years. Only relatively recently had there been any accord or agreement between them and much mutual animosity remained. It was from this period in time that the famous French saying arose – Britain would happily fight to the last Frenchman.

By 20 October the line of trenches was well established. There were to be minor alterations but the line of trenches, reaching over 400 miles from the Swiss border to the Belgian coast, remained largely unchanged until the Germans pulled back to newly prepared positions in 1917.

THE WAR IN THE EAST

As the German advance in the west stuttered to a halt, the situation in the east did not seem much better. The Russians had managed to mobilise quite speedily and by the middle of August two huge armies under generals Samsonov and Rennenkampf were already pushing towards German territory.

Early clashes led to Russian victories and the German Commander, von Prittwitz, actually considered retreat. When he heard the news, von Moltke, the Geman Commander in Chief, immediately sacked von Prittwitz and appointed the 68-year-old Paul von Hindenburg in his place. Hindenburg and his Chief of Staff, Eric Ludendorff, made a formidable team.

The two Russian armies were operating independently – indeed, their commanders were not on speaking terms and the bitter enemies had once resorted to a fist fight on a public railway station. Hindenburg and Ludendorff felt that

Above left: The idea of using art as a medium for propaganda came early in the war, after Dutch artist Louis Raemaekers published a series of drawings showing the effect of the German advance through Belgium and France. So powerful were Raemaekers' cartoons that the Germans even put a price on his head and forced him to flee to Britain.

Above right: Paul von Hindenburg, who, together with his Chief of Staff Eric Ludendorff, masterminded the great German victory over the Russians at Tannenberg.

although their forces were numerically inferior, the Russians could be attacked separately.

They fell first on Samsonov's army, on 29 August, and utterly destroyed it at the Battle of Tannenberg. They took over 90,000 prisoners, the Russian commander shooting himself in the wake of the defeat. The campaign against the more tactically adept Rennenkampf took longer, a series of battles and skirmishes unravelling along the Masurian lakes, but eventually Hindenburg and Ludendorff were successful and the Russian threat was nullified.

THE WAR AT SEA

The war at sea began badly for Britain. On the opening day of the conflict the cruiser *Amphion* was mined off the Thames Estuary and sunk. She was closely followed by the old armoured cruisers *Aboukir*, *Hogue* and *Cressy*, all torpedoed by U9 on the same day, 22 September. Seven days later the battleship *Audacious* hit a mine and also went to the bottom.

It was not all disaster for the Royal Navy, however. At the end of August Admiral Beatty and his battle cruiser squadron managed to sink three German cruisers off Heligoland Bight.

Early the following year Beatty intercepted raiding German battle cruisers. At the Battle of Dogger Bank the armoured cruiser *Bluecher* was crippled and sunk and, while the German battle cruisers managed to escape, the new *Seydlitz* was badly damaged. Beatty's *Lion* suffered heavy damage but it had been a resounding victory for the Royal Navy.

German battle cruisers twice bombarded towns on the east coast of Britain in the early war years. The damage was not great, a few windows broken in Hartlepool, Scarborough and Whitby and several people killed, but the psychological effect was huge – the sanctity of the British homeland had been shattered.

The end of the German raider *Emden*. This artist's impression of the sinking of the *Emden*, a ship that had been a thorn in the side of the British Navy for many months, is dramatic but reasonably accurate.

In August 1914 the German battle cruiser *Goeben*, accompanied by the light cruiser *Breslau*, managed to slip through the Dardanelles into Constantinople. At that stage Turkey was still neutral and the ships should have been impounded. However, a secret alliance had already been concluded between Germany and Turkey, and in November the *Goeben* led a Turkish fleet in a bombardment of Odessa and other Black Sea ports. Within days Turkey entered the war on the German side.

The light cruiser *Emden* was a thorn in the British side, roaming the Indian Ocean under the command of Captain Muller, destroying Allied merchant shipping for over three months. She was eventually hunted down and destroyed off the Cocos Islands by the Australian cruiser *Sydney* on 9 November.

The German squadron in the southern seas, under Count von Spee, consisted of four ships, including the modern armoured cruisers *Scharnhorst* and *Gneisenau*. On 1 November 1914 this squadron ran into a British force off Coronel in Chile. The British Admiral, Christopher Craddock, unwisely decided to give battle, and his old cruisers were outgunned and outfought. The British flagship *Good Hope* and the *Monmouth* were lost with all hands.

The Admiralty at once despatched two battle cruisers to the area. That December the British fleet was lying at anchor in Port Stanley on the Falkland Islands when a lookout spotted smoke on the horizon – von Spee, looking for further successes, had come, intending to attack Port Stanley. Instead he had been trapped and, in the Battle of the Falkland Islands, his fleet was utterly destroyed. In the best traditions of the German Navy, von Spee went down with his ship.

TRENCH WARFARE

As 1914 drew to a close the pattern of the war had already been mapped out. It was to be a war of hard pounding with defence always superior to attack. No matter where a breach was made, reinforcements could be quickly assembled and moved into position. Frontal attacks on well-defended positions where artillery and machine guns could dominate the battlefield were both costly and suicidal. The trouble was, the generals failed to realise it.

Trenches had been used in sieges for hundreds of years. The difference now was that a continuous line of entrenchments stretched for 400 miles across Europe, and these wet and dirty fortifications were occupied for four years of continuous warfare.

Digging and pumping water out of trenches was hard, unyielding work that, in the winter months, saw men constantly wet and covered in mud:

German soldiers take shelter as a
British shell explodes.

I have not known what it is to have a dry foot for eight days for it has been
raining day and night. The trenches get flooded and in places we have to be over
our knees in water and mud. Our sleeping places get very wet.

Private Frank Pope

Gradually, a complete and intricate trench system was created, with trenches
crawling like spiderwebs across the land – a front line, support trenches and
a reserve line – which were all joined together by communication trenches.
Sandbags protected the parapet (in front) and parados (behind) and the whole
system was guarded by yards of barbed wire.

The popular preconception of men living in the trench system for weeks and
months on end, fighting battles and charging across no man's land every day, is
false. A regular system of relief was in place, units rarely spending more than a
fortnight in the lines. The rest of the time they were out 'resting', a euphemism for
training, practising assaults and carrying supplies up to the front.

Using Territorials and Reservists to fill the gaps, by the end of the year the BEF had been extended into two powerful units, the First Army under Sir Douglas Haig and the Second Army under Sir Horace Smith-Dorrien. The BEF, still under the overall command of Sir John French, now numbered more than 270,000 men.

It was not just British soldiers serving in France. The Empire responded as enthusiastically to the call as Britain herself, and thousands of young colonials were soon in the trenches. They came in boatloads from across the oceans, eager young men coming to a land and a war that were already beyond all comprehension.

THE CHRISTMAS TRUCE OF 1914

Princess Mary's Gift Tins were freely distributed to all of the troops that first Christmas, smokers receiving an ounce of tobacco, twenty cigarettes, a pipe and a photograph of the princess. Non-smokers were given the same tin but this time it contained sweets and a writing case.

No one knew what Christmas might bring but as darkness fell on Christmas Eve, firing died away and lights began to appear above the German trenches – lanterns tied to the end of long poles. Then the Germans began to sing carols. Soon there was widespread banter and Christmas wishes were being shouted between the men on either side of no man's land.

The next day, on various parts of the line, soldiers called out to each other not to fire. Slowly men began to appear on the skyline, walking cautiously towards each other. They met in the middle of no man's land, exchanged pleasantries and mementos and even played a knock-up game of football. In some places the informal truce lasted a few hours, in others it went on all day.

Soldiers took the opportunity to bury their dead, while officers on both sides made a careful but discreet note of enemy dispositions. The truce was not universal, however, and on some parts of the line the war continued as normal. When the news reached senior officers in their headquarters at the rear there was a furious reaction.

A German Army order for 29 December made it clear that any sort of fraternisation with the British or French would be regarded as high treason, while General Smith-Dorrien quickly announced that any officer or NCO allowing friendly contact with the enemy would find themselves facing a court martial.

In general, the truce lasted just one day. On Boxing Day the war began again and death and mayhem descended once more across the Western Front. Orders soon came from High Command, on both sides of the lines, that such an event must never be allowed to happen again. In reality, it was never likely.

3

1915: AND SO IT GOES ON

New Year, 1915

For some soldiers the muted New Year celebrations were more memorable than the famous Christmas Truce. Private Frank Pope, later to become one of the casualties of war, wrote home about the moment when 1914 changed into 1915:

> At midnight on New Year's Eve we could hear them (the Germans) singing and cheering, with their band playing all the time. We were only 300 yards from them and at twelve-o-clock we started as well. We were singing to them and they to us – the Germans have got 'Tipperary' off to a treat. It was all finished up with us singing the old year out and the new one in but instead of bells we had our rifles and they had theirs – I hope I won't see the next year in here for I hope the world will be at peace before then.

Back home in Britain volunteers continued to besiege the recruiting offices. Many towns and cities pooled their volunteers into Pals battalions, units made up almost entirely of men from the same area or profession or even the same street, working on the assumption that these young men would train and fight better if they did it together. It was conveniently forgotten that they could also die together.

Life in the Trenches

Life in the trenches was cheap, death ever present. It could come suddenly, in the crash of an artillery shell or a rapid burst of machine-gun fire. It could come during one of the many trench raids ordered by High Command, raids that were supposedly designed to gain information about units in the line opposite. In reality, their main purpose was to ensure troops retained the 'offensive spirit'.

Hand grenades, originally home-made affairs created out of jam tins but soon to be properly manufactured Mills bombs, and coshes lovingly fashioned out of wood and nails were far more effective than bayonets for trench raiding. They were brutal weapons that could murder or maim in seconds.

During the day, life in the trenches was relatively low-key. Morning stand-to took place at dawn, the whole battalion coming to awareness, ready for any possible attack. This was followed by breakfast. Like all meals on the front line it was a makeshift affair, soldiers cooking tinned bacon and brewing tea on tiny 'Tommy Stoves'. Field kitchens tended to remain in reserve areas, used when a battalion was out of the line and offering soldiers a staple diet of stew.

The rest of the day was spent on fatigues, cleaning the trench areas, on rifle inspections and enjoying as much free time as men could garner. A head above the parapet could easily mean death from a sniper's shot but, for those who knew how to exploit the system, there were also benefits. There are recorded instances of soldiers deliberately holding their hands up in the air, above the sandbags that lined the front of every trench. A bullet through the palm was a guaranteed 'Blighty wound' and a trip home for a few months. The thought of a Blighty one was all that kept many soldiers sane. As the poet Robert Service wrote,

Trench mortars were hated by both sides. They were mobile weapons that could be wheeled into a trench where they would fire off a few rounds. Then the gunners would disappear to some other location, leaving the men in the lines to face to wrath and return fire of the enemy. Nevertheless, mortars were hugely effective as weapons of war.

I'm goin' 'ome to Blighty: can you wonder as I'm gay?
I've got a wound I wouldn't sell for 'alf a year o' pay.

Night time was when the lines really came alive, men creeping from their dugouts to carry out trench raids or repair the wire. It was a troglodyte existence where the normal daily routines had been totally reversed.

With the coming of night came artillery shells, huge detonations that split the air and lit the sky in red, gold and orange flashes as bright as day. Flares illuminated no man's land and the beat of machine guns on the traverse was a constant rhythm in everyone's ears. Raiding parties inched across the mud, screams and the crump of hand grenades telling where and when they had made their mark. Only with dawn did activity begin to die away.

GAS

On 22 April 1915 the Germans opened an offensive that became known as the Second Battle of Ypres. Originally intended as a minor thrust to test British and French defences, the attack soon took on more serious dimensions.

As sunset approached on 22 April, French troops to the north of Ypres saw a greenish mist creeping over the field towards them. Before long the soldiers – most of them French and Algerian – began to cough and choke. Chlorine gas had been released and soon men were streaming away from the front lines, opening up a 4-mile gap in the Allied line.

Luckily for the Allies, the Germans had made little preparation for their own troops who would, obviously, be walking into areas that had just been infected with gas. Gas masks were crude and not very effective. Despite inflicting over 15,000 casualties, the German assault began to falter as many of their own men became affected by the gas. A counter-attack by Canadian and British forces eventually saved the day. They had no gas masks but someone, sniffing at the gas and recognising it as chlorine, suggested improvised masks of handkerchiefs soaked in urine.

Soon other types of gas were also in use. Phosgene was employed to seep through the early masks, while the most deadly of them all, mustard gas, was introduced in 1917. Men on both sides lived in terror of a gas attack, knowing it could kill, maim and have many long-term effects.

AIRCRAFT

When war broke out in 1914 there were very few aircraft available and none of the opposing combatants were prepared for war in the air.

At first the RFC was treated with scepticism, but the value of aerial reconnaissance was proved when early reports on the change of direction of von Kluck's drive on Paris were sent to Army headquarters. With the trench line established, the RFC was at last able to operate from fixed, secure bases and aerial warfare moved on apace.

The value of reconnaissance and spotting of artillery fire were realised not just by the Allied generals but by the enemy as well. If there were aeroplanes up over the trenches then they needed to be destroyed before they could relay their vital information to base. And that meant anti-aircraft fire and, inevitably, fighter planes whose aim was to destroy the spotter aircraft. When fighters began to shoot down enemy fighters it brought about the beginning of dogfighting in the skies above France and Belgium.

Above left: Living in the trenches meant that lice and other bugs proliferated. This early photograph shows a machine for delousing uniforms and blankets. This was a pointless exercise, as the eggs lay dormant in the seams of the uniforms to be reactivated by body heat.

Above right: All sides had their aces, none of them more famous or successful than Manfred von Richthofen. The 'Red Baron' was the victor of eighty aerial dogfights before being shot down and killed by ground fire in 1918.

The year 1917 saw the advent of
the air ace – in Germany men like
Richthofen and Werner Voss, in
Britain people like Albert Ball and
Jimmy McCudden.

A real leap forward was achieved by Dutchman Anthony Fokker at the end of 1914. The British and the French could have secured Fokker's services but turned him down. Only the German High Command was far sighted enough to realise what the little Dutchman could bring to their war effort.

The revolutionary Fokker Eindekker was a single-winged scout plane that, due to Fokker's interrupter gear, was able to fire forward through the propeller. Using this new firing mechanism German pilots like Oswald Boelcke and Max Immelmann were soon causing chaos in the air forces of France and Britain.

By 1917 British High Command had realised the advantages of a strategic bombing campaign, and formed the Independent Air Force to attack marshalling yards and cities far beyond the lines.

Germany and France had long acclaimed their 'aces', pilots who had scored more than five aerial victories. Frenchmen like Charles Nungesser and Georges Guynemer were household names while, in Germany, aces like Boelcke and Immelmann had been superseded by men such as Werner Voss and Bruno Loerzer. Above all there was the remote but deadly Manfred von Richthofen, the famous Red Baron.

ZEPPELINS

It was not just fixed-wing aircraft that caused problems for the Allies. The first Zeppelin raid on England took place on 19 January 1915, when two airships dropped bombs on Great Yarmouth. Four people were killed, sixteen were injured and there was some limited damage to property.

Soon more raids were taking place on towns and cities across the country, London being subjected to its first raid in May. The psychological effect of the raids was immeasurable and places on the flight path of approaching Zeppelins were forced to inaugurate Britain's first blackout, turning out street and house lights in an effort to confuse the pilots.

In 1915 these massive airships seemed invincible. As they were filled with hydrogen, artillery or anti-aircraft shells could pass through the gas bags without setting the machines alight. They were big and ponderous and, in 1915, they created a reign of terror in Britain.

Zeppelin bombing of Britain stopped after 1916, when the British finally began to shoot down the cumbersome beasts. Air raids were not over, however, as bombing from fixed-wing aircraft, the enormous Gotha bombers, continued. In all, nearly 1,100 civilians in Britain died from air attack during the war.

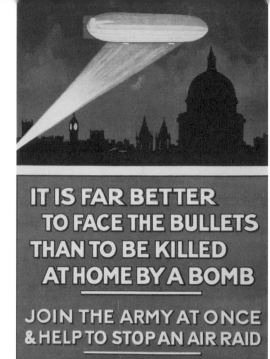

Above left and right: Zeppelins were the first 'terror weapon' of the war, quickly gaining a myth of invincibility and power. Zeppelin raids on Britain began in January 1915 and although they caused little real damage, the vision of these silent monsters nosing through banks of cloud towards their targets was enough to cause old ladies and children to tremble in their beds at night.

Below: This German drawing shows the aft compartment of a raiding Zeppelin, with gunners on the lookout for fighters and engineers working on the airship's engines.

BATTLES OF 1915

Moltke had been dismissed as Chief of the German General Staff in September 1914, the Kaiser appointing Erich von Falkenhayn in his place. He decided on a holding war in the west while he tried to break the Russians in the east. That left the French and British to take the offensive.

At the Battle of Neuve Chapelle, which began on 10 March, the BEF achieved some initial success. At this time Britain was producing just 22,000 shells per day (compared to Germany's 250,000), the problem being due partly to obsolete machinery and partly the attitude of the munitions workers, who felt that if the government wanted more shells they should pay more money.

As a result of the shortage, the preliminary bombardment at Neuve Chapelle was limited to just four hours and was hugely effective. It was a tactic that was soon forgotten, only to be revived later in the war, but at Neuve Chapelle British forces gained 1,000 yards from the Germans before the attack bogged down.

On the Eastern Front the plan for 1915 was a joint attack by the Austrians through Galicia while Hindenburg and Ludendorff advanced in the north. The Austrian attacks soon stalled but Hindenburg was more successful. In his January offensive poisonous gas was actually used for the first time. The freezing cold conditions prevented the gas spreading and it had little effect. Tragically, the Russians failed to inform their allies about the new weapon.

In February, at the Winter Battle of Masuria, where fighting took place in thick snow, Hindenburg was even more successful, inflicting 100,000 casualties on the Russians. In an effort to shore up the struggling Austrians in the south, German efforts now switched to Galicia, where the Russians were already reaching for the Carpathian Mountains. When von Mackensen smashed the Russian Army in a two-day offensive, he had effectively ended the danger of any Russian invasion of Germany.

The war in the east was far from over, however. Russia had vast untapped resources and manpower, and the war on the Eastern Front would continue to rumble on, bloody and vicious, for another two years.

THE GALLIPOLI CAMPAIGN

When Russia asked for British intervention in the Eastern Mediterranean to distract the lurking Turkish wolf, Churchill, First Lord of the Admiralty, and Jacky Fisher, then First Sea Lord, thought something might be done in the Dardanelles, the narrow waterway connecting the Mediterranean to the Black Sea. They took the idea to Prime Minister Asquith and it was agreed. An assault would be made on the Dardanelles.

The entrance to the Dardanelles was covered by a huge array of guns, minefields and searchlights. Further batteries of guns lined the cliffs, and with the width of the channel at its narrowest point being just 1,600 yards, this was always going to be a dangerous operation.

From the beginning the campaign was a disastrous muddle. Churchill was convinced that the Royal Navy could destroy the forts without any assistance. Indeed, they had already been bombarded in November 1914, an action that had no effect other than to alert the Turks to what was to come. Further bombardments took place on 19 February 1915 and this time many of the forts were destroyed. Marines landed to mop up the dazed Turkish soldiers and to blow up any remaining defence works.

And there things stopped. Amazingly, despite the success of the operation, nothing happened for another month. The defenders – German General Liman von Sanders and Mustafa Kemal, later Kemal Ataturk – rushed extra forces to the area. When, in March, the naval forces moved warily down the straits, they ran into a minefield. Three old battleships were sunk and several more were damaged. They promptly withdrew to Alexandria. This time there was a delay of two months.

The British Commander in Chief, Sir Ian Hamilton, a patient and good-natured man, was too old and not really suited to the task. Loading and reloading the transports to his satisfaction took weeks, and when his preparations were eventually complete Hamilton's five divisions of British and Anzac troops (the Australian and New Zealand Army Corps) were matched by those of the Turks.

Even so, Hamilton's landings at Kumkale, Cape Helles and Anzac Cove on the western side of the Gallipoli Peninsula took the Turks by surprise. At all landing sites the troops got ashore, but then they encountered fierce opposition that pinned them down on the beaches. Hamilton remained on board ship, out of touch with his troops and with events as they unfolded.

To relieve the pressure another landing was made, at Suvla Bay in the north of the peninsula. The Gurkhas did manage to fight their way off the beach and climb to the top of the ridge, looking down on the open waters of the Dardanelles. The battleships offshore spotted the figures, but did not believe that Allied troops could have penetrated so far inland. They promptly opened fire and the Gurkhas were forced to retreat to the beach. Never again did Allied forces manage to breach the Turkish lines.

By the autumn of 1915 it was clear that the Gallipoli Campaign had turned into a disaster on a massive scale. No matter how many extra troops were sent, they were always matched by Turkish replacements and it proved impossible to get the men off the beaches.

Sir Ian Hamilton was relieved and replaced by General Monro, but when Field Marshal Kitchener visited the scene he was appalled by what he saw. His report to the High Command was simple – the Gallipoli Campaign must be called off.

Evacuation began in December 1915 and ended, with the last troops taken off the beach at Suvla Bay, on 9 January 1916. It was a hugely effective withdrawal, in utter contrast to the rest of the campaign. The Turks did not even realise the enemy was leaving until they woke one morning to find the beaches and trenches opposite them totally empty.

Nearly 500,000 Allied troops had been involved in the landings and occupation of Gallipoli, 250,000 of them becoming casualties. Many of those casualties came through disease rather than enemy action.

In this wake, Churchill was forced to resign from the Admiralty. Having served as a soldier in the Sudan under Kitchener, he was able to gain a commission in the Army and within a few weeks he was in command of the 6th Battalion, Royal Scots Fusiliers. 'I came, I saw, I capitulated' was his final comment on the affair.

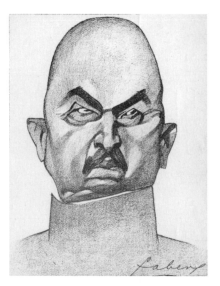

Above left: A cartoon showing German general von Sanders, one of the masterminds behind the Turkish defence of Gallipoli.

Above right: Allied troops bathing in the sea during one of the rare moments of peace in the Gallipoli Campaign. It was not always this quiet – the Turkish batteries often shelled soldiers as they washed and bathed.

Admiral Jacky Fisher also went. Convinced he was irreplaceable, he wrote a virulent letter to Prime Minister Asquith, outlining the things he would need if he was going to stay as First Sea Lord. Travelling north to his home in Scotland, he was met by the station master on the platform at Crewe with a telegram – Asquith had accepted his resignation.

The battles on the Gallipoli Peninsula exacted a terrible cost in human life. The Anzac forces never forgave the ineptitude of the British generals, men who had condemned them to death and disaster, but for the ordinary soldier – British, Australian, New Zealander – the real heroes of the campaign were the men who had fought and died on those terrible beaches.

> Above your graves no wattle blooms
> Nor flowers from English dells,
> You men who sleep uneasily
> Beside the Dardanelles.

Much of the general perception about the running of the war comes from the sheer ineptitude of the men in charge of the Gallipoli Campaign. The idea was right, the execution totally wrong.

THE SALONIKA CAMPAIGN

Bulgaria joined the war in September 1915, coming in on the side of Germany. Almost immediately the Bulgarians launched an assault on Serbia.

The Allies saw the manoeuvrings in the Balkans as a direct threat on Greece. A force of one French and two British divisions was assembled under French general Maurice Sarrail, and quickly moved from Gallipoli to Salonika (now known as Thessalonica) in order to defend and protect Greek territory.

The aim was for this Allied force to move off its beachhead, to link up with the Serbs and push back the enemy forces. Unfortunately, the Bulgarians had established a commanding position astride the main communication routes, a position from where they were eventually able to roll up the Serbian forces and push them towards the sea.

The Serbs, along with over 20,000 Austrian prisoners, fell back over rugged mountain terrain in what became an epic retreat. Over half the Serbian Army perished in the horrendous conditions before being picked up off the beaches by French boats. With their army gone, Serbia and most of the Balkans lay wide open and the Austrians quickly overran Montenegro.

The Allied army in Salonika found itself isolated and with little purpose. However, General Sarrail dared not evacuate, knowing that would leave Greece wide open to attack. As a consequence the army simply wired itself in, hoping that its presence alone would be enough to deter an assault. It was a hard, cruel existence. In the early days troops slept in their greatcoats, lying in holes dug in the ground. By morning these coats would be full of water – and then the sun came up. Sunstroke or frostbite, they could both kill.

The Germans scathingly called the Allied enclosure the biggest internment camp in Europe. They knew that valuable Allied forces were tied up here rather than fighting on the Western Front.

ITALY ENTERS THE WAR

On the outbreak of war, despite being a member of the Triple Alliance – Germany, Austria-Hungary and Italy – Italy announced that joining the conflict did not come within her remit. She promptly declared herself neutral.

With both sides needing allies, a bizarre auction process began, with everyone competing for the support and help of countries like Bulgaria and Italy. The Allies even offered Italy land in the Austrian Tyrol, the city of Trieste and more territory in Asia Minor if she would come in on their side.

The country's leaders knew that if Italy had any ambitions to be a great power she would have to take part in the conflict. On 26 April 1915 Italy signed the secret Treaty of London, promising to enter the war within the month. True to their word, on 23 May the Italian government declared war on Austria-Hungary. Yet they did not feel able to take on the might of Germany and it was not until August 1916 that Italy finally went to war with the Germans.

The Italians planned to invade the Austro-Hungarian plain, but first they had to get over the mountains. The Battle of Isonzo, in reality eleven different but linked battles, took place between June and November 1915. Little was gained, but as many as 160,000 casualties were incurred in what was a bloodbath on both sides, and here, as elsewhere, the war ground on relentlessly.

THE SUEZ CANAL

A Turkish thrust towards the Suez Canal in February 1915 caused consternation in British ranks. Britain could not afford to lose control of the canal as it was the main route to and from India. So when 20,000 Turkish soldiers suddenly appeared out of the Sinai Desert, there was panic.

Luckily the attack was repulsed fairly easily. The British High Command had learned a lesson, however, and reinforcements were immediately sent to the region. In the event the Turks did not try for the canal again for another eighteen months.

The cost of maintaining a garrison in this part of Egypt was immense, and the soldiers who were sitting on the Suez Canal could and should have been of more use in France. It was an interesting experience for many of the young soldiers.

I'd joined up expecting to be in France, on the Western Front, in a few weeks but, instead, I found myself in Egypt. I'd read about the pyramids and now, suddenly, there they were in front of me. It was amazing. For me the most impressive thing was the Sphinx. It just sat there in the desert like a giant cat. I was shocked, taken aback. This thing had been there for thousands of years and here we were, knowing that sooner or later we would be facing death and destruction.

Conversation with Robert Turnbull Carradice, transcript held by author

For the young soldiers Egypt was a brief interlude, and most moved on to Gallipoli or France. For some it would be the country where they waited, impatient and frustrated, until the campaigns in Mesopotamia and Palestine began in earnest.

MESOPOTAMIA

In an attempt to protect British oil interests in the Middle East, a British and Indian force was landed in Mesopotamia (modern-day Iraq but then part of the Turkish Empire) in the autumn of 1914. Basra was soon occupied, and the decision was made to press northwards and occupy the whole country.

General Townshend reached Kut al Amira in September and took the town fairly easily. With extended lines of communication, he was dubious about pressing on. Another victory at Ctesiphon left Townshend's force so exhausted that he had no option but to retire to Kut. And there his command of 9,000 men was besieged by a superior force of Turks.

Several attempts were made to relieve the men at Kut, but all were unsuccessful. Townshend held out for several months before, in April 1916, with supplies running out, he was forced to surrender. The garrison was marched off into captivity; 5,000 of the 9,000 men were never heard of again.

Above left: The Balkans became something of a forgotten theatre of the war, but the fighting here was as fierce as anything on the Western or Eastern Fronts.

Above right: Success of the war in the Middle East was vital for the protection of Britain's oil interests.

THE WAR IN AFRICA

German colonies in Africa were captured quite quickly once war began, Togoland and the Cameroons being in Allied hands by the end of February 1915. The assault on German South West Africa (now Namibia) took a little longer, mainly due to a rebellion in the South African forces deployed for the campaign. Despite this, by July 1915, German forces had surrendered to Louis Botha.

Little progress was made in East Africa, however. Here the German commander was the inventive Paul von Lettow-Vorbeck. The terrain over which the war was fought consisted of thick brush, and von Lettow-Vorbeck's mainly African askaris were experts in dealing with such difficult territory.

Finally, the government of South Africa appointed General Smuts, a Boer War guerrilla commander of some note, to deal with von Lettow-Vorbeck. Even so, it was not until the middle of 1916 that Dar-es-Salaam was captured, and even then Von Lettow-Vorbeck escaped to continue the fight.

The war in Africa was something of a stop–go affair, but German General Paul von Lettow-Vorbeck managed to keep British forces at bay for several years.

THE *LUSITANIA* AND NURSE CAVELL

Early in 1915 Germany declared a blockade of the British Isles. It was a warning to all ships, of whatever nationality, that if they came within sight or range of a U-boat they would be destroyed without compunction. Calls of 'German barbarity' counted for nothing.

When the liner *Lusitania* was sighted by U20 off the coast of Ireland in March 1915 she was too good a target to miss, and a single torpedo sent her to the bottom. Ostensibly a vessel carrying just passengers, the speed with which the ship broke up and a secondary explosion on board soon after the torpedo struck does seem to indicate that she was also carrying explosives or military supplies.

Unfortunately, 1,195 men and women also went down with the *Lusitania*, 128 of them being American citizens. President Wilson protested and it quickly became clear to men like the German chancellor Theobald Bethmann-Hollweg that such indignation could even bring America into the war. As a result, the German 'sink at sight' campaign was abandoned, or at least severely limited until the idea of 'total war' was adopted in 1916.

On 11 October 1915 Edith Cavell was executed by the Germans in Brussels. She had been working as the matron of Berkendael Institute, a school for nurses,

Above left: The torpedoing of the *Lusitania* brought an immediate outcry. For a while it seemed as if America could enter the war.

Above right: Nurse Edith Cavell, shot by the Germans as someone who had been helping enemy soldiers to escape. The execution brought further condemnation of 'barbaric' German policies.

and here she first shielded and then helped British and French soldiers to escape to neutral Holland. Arrested and put on trial, she was condemned to death, not as a spy but as someone who had helped enemy soldiers to escape. Protests from all over the world could not save her.

THE BATTLE OF LOOS

The Battle of Loos in September 1915 was the biggest battle that the British Army had fought, up to that time. It was also one of the biggest disasters and it spelled the end of the line for the commander of the British Expeditionary Force, Sir John French.

At 6.30 a.m. on 26 September, gas was released and British troops went over the top. In a swirling wind the gas drifted forward on the right but swept backwards on the left, asphyxiating many of the attacking troops. And when they reached the German lines soldiers found the wire uncut by the bombardment. In fierce fighting the village of Loos was taken by Haig's First Army, but the reserves did not appear in time and the gains were quickly lost. French, never Haig's greatest friend or colleague, simply did not trust him to use his forces appropriately and therefore kept the reserves under his own command.

Despite Haig's urgent demands for support, it was not until mid-morning that the reserves were finally released. By then the Germans had managed to regroup and the advancing men were mown down by machine guns that traversed along the line of troops. In just four hours over 4,000 soldiers were killed, total British losses for the battle amounting to 43,000.

Sir John French was severely criticised by many officers, among them Douglas Haig. Haig had the ear of the king and was determined that blame for the failure should lie at the door of French, not him. He also had designs on Sir John's job, and even went so far as to circulate 'leaked' papers regarding French's handling of the reserves. It was underhand behaviour, but it worked.

French's position had become untenable and he was eventually relieved in December 1915. When the reshuffling had finished, French found himself replaced by none other than Sir Douglas Haig.

Change in the Air

It wasn't just Sir John French, Churchill and Fisher who went to the wall. In the wake of failures in France and the chaos of the Gallipoli Campaign, H. H. Asquith, the Liberal Prime Minister, realised his position was tenuous. He decided that the only way forward was to form a coalition government with the Conservatives.

Lloyd George became Minister for Munitions. The man of the people, as he liked to style himself, quickly persuaded the unions to end their restrictions on quantity of shell production. Working conditions and fixed wages could be dealt with after the war, Lloyd George promised. In the meantime, let's get on with the job.

The suffragettes had suspended their political protests in 1914 but they had been wanting, for some time, the right to work alongside men. Lloyd George now gave them that right. Thousands of women were brought into the armaments factories, their smaller hands being particularly useful for reaching down inside shell casings.

Soon women were working at a whole range of jobs that had previously been closed to them. They drove busses and trams, worked on farms and delivered coal. There were even, for the first time, women police officers. As 1915 came to an end it was clear that the world had changed – and this time it had changed for ever.

4

1916: THE YEAR OF SLAUGHTER

CONSCRIPTION

On 6 January 1916 the British government broke with hundreds of years of tradition and introduced a Bill to bring in compulsory military service for all single men.

The expected disapproval of the Liberal Party did not materialise and the Bill quickly became enshrined in law. Voluntary recruiting stopped but, rather than catching the half million 'shirkers' that the Act was expected to expose, almost immediately there were over a million claims from men who wanted exemption because they were engaged in essential war work.

A new phenomenon also suddenly appeared – the conscientious objector. Now that service in the armed forces was compulsory, men were able to object to the war on moral and religious grounds. There were not many of these objectors, perhaps 5,000 in total but, by and large, they were treated harshly by the authorities. Many of them were imprisoned for their beliefs, sentenced to hard labour in Dartmoor and other prisons.

One thing that conscription did end was underage enlistment. So many young boys had lied about their age in order to join up. When they reached the front it was only understandable when some of them were unable to cope with the horror and brutality of what they saw. In all, 346 British soldiers were shot by firing squads during the war, the vast majority (266 of them) for desertion in the face of the enemy. Conscription would not end this process, but it would cut out the needless suffering of young lads whose only real mistake was that they had been 'ardent for some desperate glory'.

Once conscription had been introduced, it was perhaps inevitable that the terms by which it operated should be extended. The original legislation had been aimed only at single men over the age of eighteen. However, in May 1916 this was extended to cover married men as well.

THE BATTLE OF VERDUN

By 1916 'Papa' Joffre was insistent that a joint offensive, British and French, would break the German armies and the place to unroll this attack was not in Flanders, but in the relatively unspoiled and unmarked Somme region. Britain had not been pulling her weight, Joffre felt, and what he wanted now was to involve Haig and his armies in heavy fighting.

Haig, acting under instructions from Kitchener, acquiesced to Joffre's request and the two generals began to plan for the attack. Unfortunately they were

A French ammunition convoy makes its way along the Sacred Way, the only route into the besieged town of Verdun, around 1916.

British soldiers, complete with equipment to replace and repair barbed wire, make their way to the front during the Battle of the Somme.

forestalled, as von Falkenhayn was also planning an assault. Falkenhayn was aware of the casualties France had suffered during the past eighteen months and was convinced that if he could bleed the French Army dry then it would deprive Britain of her ally and thus shorten the war by many months.

Falkenhayn needed a target that was a symbol, the loss of which would destroy the morale of the French nation. He found it in the fortress city of Verdun. Even though the forts of Verdun were already redundant, the French people did not realise this – to them they were a symbol of French pride and military efficiency.

The attack began on 21 February 1916, an enormous bombardment that could be heard 50 miles away. The forts and the town were reduced to rubble, but the French line held. Despite the fact that Verdun was of little strategic value Joffre ordered that there should be no retreat, and thus fell happily into Falkenhayn's trap.

What ensued was a bloodbath, as both sides fought to a standstill. The French commander, General Henri Petain, and his subordinate Robert Nivelle, were inspirational as the Germans threw themselves against the defences. 'They shall not pass' was the cry, willingly and eagerly taken up by the men in the trenches.

This was a battle of attrition, where the victor would be the side who could endure the longest. To do this, supplies of weapons and reinforcements were essential. The German forces had good rail and road links behind their lines; the French had just one way into the city, a road that soon became known as La Voie Sacrée (The Sacred Way). Along this 75-mile track nearly 3,000 lorries and carts passed each day, carrying 50,000 tons of munitions and supplies.

When fighting finally died away at the end of June, the French had suffered over 400,000 casualties. The Germans had lost nearly 350,000. It was a senseless battle with no objective other than to wear down the other side. In the end it was a victory, of sorts, for the French. They had, more or less, held their ground, but Falkenhayn never knew how close he had come to his objective. Verdun destroyed the spirit of the French Army and the mutinies that broke out later in the year were directly related to the horror of this senseless, mindless bloodbath.

THE BATTLE OF THE SOMME

Joffre's original intention had been to launch a combined British and French offensive on the Somme in the summer of 1916. Clearly this could not now happen and Haig, bowing to pressure from the French, agreed to mount an attack with predominantly British forces.

Haig had become convinced that this undamaged and gently rolling pasture land was the spot where the war could be won. British forces were moved into the area, most of them men of Kitchener's New Army. This was to be their blooding and they, like Haig, were convinced that they would succeed where others before them had failed.

However, the Germans held all the high ground and, more significantly, because there had been so little action in the area they had had the time to construct deep dugouts in the chalky soil. These dugouts made them almost immune to any type of shelling available to the British in 1916.

The attack on 1 July 1916 was preceded by a bombardment on a colossal scale, lasting for a total of five days. Observers from the Royal Flying Corps reported widespread devastation but they, and the generals, did not realise that whatever damage might be inflicted on the first and second lines of trenches, the Germans were waiting, safe and sound, in their deep dugouts.

When the shelling stopped the men of Kitchener's New Army went over the top, walking forward in regular lines, shoulder to shoulder, waving flags and singing their interminable soldiers' songs. Each of them carried 60 lbs of equipment on his back, and the ground over which they walked had been turned into a quagmire by the shelling. The barbed wire, however, remained largely uncut, and this was where the German machine gunners caught them. The attack had begun at 7.30 a.m., and before most people in Britain had even finished their breakfast, over 14,000 men had been killed.

In hindsight, the Somme was a disaster waiting to happen. The men of the New Army had received scant training. They knew how to walk forward in a line and how to use the bayonet on a demoralised foe, but little else. Their junior officers were brave and, like their men, full of reckless enthusiasm. They had been told to lead from the front, to expose themselves to enemy fire – as an example – and so were often mown down in the first moments of the battle.

The first day of the Somme was the worst day in the history of the British Army. The casualty figure of 57,470 included nearly 20,000 killed.

Once the initial shock had worn off, British High Command had to consider what to do next. Everyone thought the Germans must be close to breaking point. Therefore the battle should continue. Over the next few months numerous attacks – all loosely grouped together under the title of the Battle of the Somme – were made on positions like Delville and Mametz woods. The attack on Mametz Wood by the 38th (Welsh) Division was a particularly brutal affair that was meant to take less than a day. The battle lasted five days and destroyed the Welsh Division as a fighting force.

The final attack took place on 13 November, when the village of Beaumont Hamel was eventually taken, and thereafter both sides subsided into a daze of recrimination and wonder. British casualties for the battle amounted to 420,000. Even the French, who had occupied a small portion of the southern front, lost 205,000. German losses came to over 600,000.

If, as has sometimes been claimed, the Somme was 'the death of an army' – meaning Kitchener's New Army – it also has to be seen as the death of the old German Army. Old values and old positions died along with the soldiers on the Somme.

REBELLION IN IRELAND

When war broke out in 1914 most Irishmen, Protestant and Catholic alike, immediately rallied to the British flag. For most, the long-standing issue of Home Rule was suspended until hostilities were over. However, a small number of partisans quickly realised that Britain, engaged in a life-and-death struggle with Germany, was suddenly vulnerable. This was their chance.

On Easter Monday members of the Irish Volunteers, supported by the Irish Citizen Army, seized strategic buildings around Dublin, notably the post office in Sackville Street. From here they proclaimed a new Irish Republic. When British troops were sent to calm the situation, fighting broke out and lasted for five days.

During the coming week the rebels were reinforced by 1,600 volunteers. Eventually almost 20,000 British troops were facing them in the Dublin streets. Artillery was brought in to bombard the post office and eleven people were killed before the rebels finally surrendered.

The men who had signed the proclamation, and many of the Volunteer commandants, were executed by firing squad. James Connolly, too badly injured to walk, was carried out into the execution yard in a chair. Idealists like Patrick Pearse and James Plunkett wanted death and martyrdom, as they felt only in this way could the spirit of Irish nationalism be brought alive once more. Foolishly, the British authorities gave them what they wanted.

By executing so many of the leaders, the British government made the rebels – most of whom were unpopular at the time, even in their homeland being viewed as unpatriotic – into heroes. In effect, the British had turned Ireland into a hotbed of republicanism and rebellion. It was something which, in years to come, would come back to haunt them, many times.

TOTAL WAR

In the wake of Verdun and the Somme it was clear that Falkenhayn had shot his bolt. On 29 August, with both battles still raging, he was replaced as Chief of the General Staff by Paul von Hindenburg, the victor of the Eastern Front. Hindenburg came accompanied by Ludendorff – and both men knew that the only route to victory was by the concept of 'total war'.

Ludendorff was undoubtedly the power behind von Hindenburg's new throne. He was sometimes known as 'Hindenburg's Brain' and was an adherent to the ideas of nineteenth-century strategist Karl von Clausewitz.

Von Clausewitz had been clear that the only way to defeat an enemy was to smash him utterly, to grind him into the dirt – in other words, 'total war'. Now Ludendorff was about to put the ideas and theories of von Clausewitz into terrible practice.

THE BATTLE OF JUTLAND

It has been said that Admiral Sir John Jellicoe, commander of the British Grand Fleet, was the only man who could lose the war in a single afternoon. The responsibility of controlling and directing Britain's greatest weapon was indeed a heavy one.

At the end of May 1916, Admiral Scheer, commander of the German High Seas Fleet, decided that he had lain inactive long enough and sent out his battle-cruiser squadron under Admiral Hipper in the direction of the Skagerrak Straits, knowing that the move was bound to attract the attention of the British.

What emerged was a massive game of cat and mouse. Scheer was hoping to lure Admiral Beatty's ships beneath the guns of his battleships; Jellicoe, thundering in the wake of Beatty's battle cruisers, was hoping to catch the Germans in their own trap. There had never been a greater gathering of warships. On the British side there were twenty-eight dreadnought battleships, nine battle cruisers. The German High Seas Fleet consisted of twenty-two battleships, five battle cruisers.

The battle began just before 4.00 p.m. on 31 May when the two battle-cruiser squadrons sighted each other off Jutland. As planned, Hipper immediately wheeled around and set off back to the security of the guns promised by the High Seas Fleet. Beatty followed.

British gunnery was markedly inferior to that of the Germans, and it soon became apparent that Beatty was in trouble. Two of his ships, the *Indefatigable* and the *Queen Mary*, blew up and sank, lost with virtually all hands, while his own flagship,

Lion, was seriously damaged. It led Beatty to turn to his flag captain and utter his classic line, 'There seems to be something wrong with our bloody ships today.'

Indeed there was. Quite apart from their poor gunnery, it was common practice in the Royal Navy to leave open the doors to the ammunition hoists when in action. Shells and cordite were stacked in open companionways to facilitate quicker firing. All of this was fine, but when hit by shells it could lead to flash explosions that could destroy a ship in seconds.

It was not all one-way traffic, Beatty managing to sink the *Von der Tann* and cripple three other battle cruisers, but as dusk fell the two main battle fleets finally came within range of each other. As the British battleships opened fire, Scheer suddenly realised the danger and turned away, but not before sinking another battle cruiser, the *Invincible*. Jellicoe, only too aware of submarines and mines, also withdrew and headed back to port.

The British lost more ships in the battle – three battle cruisers, three cruisers and eight destroyers. In contrast the Germans lost one battleship, one battle cruiser, four cruisers and five destroyers. But strategically, Jutland was a clear

The Battle of Jutland, fought on 31 May 1916, was the only occasion that the British and German fleets came face to face, apart from November 1918, when the High Seas Fleet came out to surrender. This German postcard shows the German fleet and its commander, Admiral Scheer.

British victory. Scheer knew how close he had come to disaster, and the High Seas Fleet never again ventured out in anger. Britain still ruled the waves and clearly Germany did not. As a consequence, the British blockade of Germany was tightened, a tactic that ultimately contributed greatly to Allied victory in the war.

The Submarine Threat

One of the major consequences of the Battle of Jutland was the Germans' final realisation that they could not defeat Britain at sea, at least not using traditional capital ships. They knew that if there was ever to be another Jutland there could only be one winner.

Sailors were taken from the High Seas Fleet to be trained as submariners, and before the year was out the U-boat threat had become very real. The effect of the U-boat campaign was phenomenal. The average total of Allied merchant ships lost to submarines during 1916 rose dramatically from less than 90,000 tons a month to 190,000, a total that threatened to grow and overwhelm the always fragile infrastructure of any island nation.

There was, even at this early stage, one way to defeat the U-boat menace – convoys. Yet the Admiralty was strangely reluctant to introduce the system, believing that it would simply give the submarines a greater number of targets to aim at. And so, for the time being, cargo vessels were left to plough their lonely furrows across the world's oceans, trusting to luck and good judgement.

Christmas in the Trenches

The Christmas Truce of 1914 was never repeated, but the Christmas period was the one time of the year when soldiers on both sides of no man's land looked forward to a few moments of extra comfort. The front lines still needed to be held, but there was often little activity in the trenches at this time.

Christmas dinner – even if conditions forced it to be taken a day or so late – meant good food: beef and plum pudding instead of the usual stew. It was something to be looked forward to with relish.

Christmas cards and postcards were produced by UK publishers, usually with a humorous but pointed message – it might be Christmas but there was still a war to be won. German postcards tended to be far more traditional, emphasising humanity and good will to all (though not, of course, to the enemy).

A German Christmas card shows a soldier in a pickelhaube helmet making his way back to his dugout, complete with seasonal provisions and Christmas tree.

Father Christmas visits German troops, bringing presents, parcels and good wishes.

Many regiments produced their own Christmas cards. These were sent by the soldiers to loved ones at home, and the cards often showed the battle honours of the particular regiment. Even prisoners of war produced their own Christmas cards and, amazingly, these were sent and received by families at home.

CHANGES AT THE TOP

As 1916 ground to a close, changes were afoot in several different spheres. That October General Nivelle, one of the French heroes of Verdun, had become a national hero when he retook much of the territory that had been lost to Germany in the earlier battle. Nivelle claimed that he had found the secret of victory and, although he resolutely refused to disclose quite what the secret was, the French people were desperate enough to clutch at any straw, however slight it might be.

'Papa' Joffre was promoted to Marshal of France and 'pushed upstairs'. He had had a good innings but had failed to win the war. Now it was someone else's turn. Nivelle succeeded him as commander on the Western Front.

In Britain there was much speculation about the conduct of the war, which, everyone agreed, was not going well. Lloyd George, always an arch conspirator, was at the heart of the debate, and he was supported by the Conservative leader Andrew Bonar Law. That November, in something of a palace coup, they suggested that Asquith might like to remain as Prime Minister but that conduct of the war should rest in the hands of none other than Lloyd George. Asquith, after first seeming to agree, soon changed his mind and broke up the coalition government. His plan was to reform his cabinet without Lloyd George.

As a political move it was a disaster. Most MPs also wanted a more energetic and dynamic running of the war and, having seemingly got rid of Asquith, they were not going to let him back in. Lloyd George was their man. With support from both Liberals and Conservatives, he duly became Prime Minister on 7 December 1916.

Lloyd George immediately set up a war cabinet of five men – a small, powerful cabal with the power and determination to take unpleasant but necessary decisions. They were men who had no other departmental duties, men who could concentrate on winning the war. If necessary they would bring in businessmen and trade unionists to advise and help. It had been a long, hard road, but at last Britain had got the leadership she deserved, a leadership that might just win the war.

Allied commanders Joffre, Foch and Haig stand for their photograph with King George of Britain and President Poincaré of France.

5
1917: MUD AND BLOOD

THE HINDENBURG LINE

Having taken command of the German forces in the west, Hindenburg and Ludendorff realised there was a need to shorten their line. During the winter of 1916/17 a new set of trenches, several miles behind the original ones, was cut across the base of a salient that had previously bulged out into Allied territory. When it was complete, the new line, known by the British as the Hindenburg Line, shortened the German front line by almost 35 miles.

It consisted of purpose-built trenches, amazing pieces of military architecture that were designed to house soldiers, equipment and supplies for years if necessary.

Concrete bunkers and deep tunnels for the movement of troops between one spot on the line and another were just part of the system. There were also concrete machine-gun emplacements with wide arcs of fire and roll upon roll of barbed wire. In front of the line were fortified outpost villages, carefully designed to give covering fire to each other.

In February 1917 the German Army began to withdraw to these carefully prepared lines. The land between the old front and the new one was deliberately obliterated, a scorched earth policy that left just open fields of mud that any attacking force would now have to cross.

REVOLUTION IN RUSSIA

From September 1915 the Czar had taken personal charge of running Russia's war. He was often away from home, at the front, directing operations that should have been left to his generals – and not directing them particularly well.

That left his wife, Czarina Alexandra, to take charge of domestic affairs at the Russian court. Influenced by the mystic monk Gregory Rasputin, who seemed to have the power to help her haemophiliac son, Alexandra made stupid blunders, dismissing court officials who could have been offering realistic advice. Being of

Sketches of Tommy's life Out on rest — Nº 2

As you are supposed to be resting in a quiet spot, a litt'e light literature goes well.

One of a series of comic postcards drawn by Canadian artist Fergus Mackain, depicting scenes from the life of a British soldier. Hugely popular with the soldiers because of their authenticity, these cards were collected in their dozens and sent back home to family and friends.

German origin, there was a great dislike of Alexandra in the country, and when the ordinary man or woman looked at the corruption and opulence of the Czar's court they could be excused for asking who was making all the sacrifices in the war.

In early March strikes and serious food riots broke out in Petrograd. Mobs charged along the streets and broke into the prisons, releasing many of the political prisoners who had been held in captivity. There was open criticism of the Czar and the Duma, the Russian Parliament, refused his orders to disband.

Czar Nicholas, finally realising there was chaos in his capital, attempted to leave the front and return to Petrograd. Railway workers stopped his train and forced him back to military headquarters. Faced by revolution from the people, his generals advised abdication. Reluctantly, Nicholas agreed. The Romanov dynasty that had ruled Russia for hundreds of years had collapsed in a matter of weeks.

A new, liberal government was set up, headed by the lawyer Alexander Kerensky. Even then, ominous stirrings could be seen in the shape of socialist peoples' groups known as Soviets, which, in the wake of the Czar's departure, had been established. Slowly, they increased their power over the things that mattered to the population – food, fuel and effective local government. But at this stage Kerensky was clear: there was no intention of leaving the war. The Czar was blamed for the bad running of the country and its war effort. His liberal government would do better.

The German leadership soon realised that Kerensky intended to continue fighting alongside France and Britain. The revolutionary Lenin, leader of Russia's Bolshevik faction, had fled the country many years before and was living in exile in Switzerland. As a Marxist, his long-stated aim was to create a system of international socialism, but he also believed that if Russia withdrew from the conflict other warring nations would soon follow its lead.

Ludendorff, increasingly the real power in Germany, seized on Lenin's words and provided him with a sealed train to travel into Russia. He also gave Lenin money to help with the second revolution that he hoped would occur once the Bolshevik leader was back in Russia. True to his word, Lenin arrived in Petrograd on 16 April 1917 and within a few days denounced the new provisional government. There, joined by fellow revolutionary Leon Trotsky, he began preaching revolution.

AMERICA ENTERS THE WAR

In line with the concept of 'total war', Germany announced the introduction of unrestricted submarine warfare at the end of January 1917. From now on, all shipping – Allied or neutral – would be sunk on sight if it was found in the eastern Atlantic. Hindenburg and Ludendorff believed the policy, effectively starving Britain to death, would bring them victory within six months. In reality it was one of the major factors that brought the USA into the war and, eventually, spelled German defeat.

The idea of unrestricted submarine warfare was abhorrent to the Americans, not just because of the loss of innocent life, but because so many American ships, loaded with valuable goods, would now either be sunk or, fearing what might await them in the Atlantic, remain tied up in port. Either way there was likely to be a huge loss of revenue for American businessmen.

Since the start of war huge quantities of wheat, cotton and raw materials for industry had been streaming across the Atlantic. It was not just the capitalist businessmen who had made themselves fortunes. Wages were high, factories worked overtime – it was certainly a time of plenty for all Americans. Now the spectre of war inched closer.

Above left: Russian soldiers in action on the Eastern Front. A romantic view but, even in this artist-drawn postcard, their uniforms and clothing can hardly have been appropriate for the conditions.

Above right: No man's land after a battle, as seen by official war artist C. R. W. Nevinson.

The immediate cause of the USA joining the war, however, was the Zimmerman Telegram. On 16 January the German Foreign Secretary, Arthur Zimmerman, sent an ill-advised telegram to the Mexican government. In it he proposed that in return for Mexico joining Germany in an alliance, there would be huge rewards. Once the war was won, Germany would help Mexico to regain Texas, New Mexico and Arizona. It was a fatuous offer. There was no way Germany could ever back up such an offer and, anyway, the Mexicans had no desire to declare war on the USA.

The telegram was intercepted by the British government and, eventually, the full text was printed in the American newspapers. It was all that President Woodrow Wilson needed. On 6 April 1917 the USA declared war on Germany. It would be several months before America could put an army into the field, the first 14,000 doughboys arriving in France that August. But Germany's worst fear had been realised; America had joined the Allies.

THE BATTLE OF ARRAS

In an attempt to distract German attention from French preparations for the so-called Nivelle Offensive, Field Marshal Haig had allowed himself to be persuaded that it was time for British troops to attack again. This time the area chosen was at Arras.

The Battle of Arras began on 9 April with the now customary bombardment. And to begin with there was considerable success. The Canadians of the First Army took Vimy Ridge, capturing many guns and prisoners in the process. After an advance of 5 miles, the attack ground to a halt in front of the Hindenburg Line. This was where the Battle of Arras should have ended, but the thought of the final breakthrough was too great for a cavalryman like Haig.

On 23 April the attacks began again and this time, with no element of surprise, they achieved nothing. The Germans had brought up reserves and were ready. The Battle of Arras cost Britain 150,000 casualties, among them the poet Edward Thomas, who was killed by the blast of an artillery shell in the opening moments of the battle. German casualties amounted to 100,000.

THE NIVELLE OFFENSIVE

General Nivelle, the man who had claimed to hold the secret to winning the war, launched his offensive on the River Aisne on 16 April. Nivelle might well have had the secret, but his plan of campaign was already known to the Germans. A French NCO (non-commissioned officer) had been captured with full details of the attack in his coat pocket – although quite why a lowly NCO should have such details about his person has never been properly explained.

The early stages of the battle had been marred for the French by the German scorched earth policy and the land the soldiers had to cross was a quagmire of mud and booby traps. As ever, the preliminary bombardment was ineffective, failing to break the wire and serving only to churn up the ground even more. The Germans were sheltering deep underground until the bombardment ended and then, when the French soldiers advanced, they walked into a hail of machine-gun fire.

The French lost 96,000 men and instead of gaining 6 miles, as Nivelle had boasted, the gain was a paltry 600 yards. Nivelle had promised that the battle would be over in two days. In the event it lasted two weeks and then simply faded into the normal routine of trench warfare.

At the end of the month, before the final echoes of his great offensive had even died away, Nivelle was replaced by Henri Petain, the hero of Verdun, who was

WAR POETRY

From the beginning of the war, poets had tried to put their thoughts and feelings about the conflict into words. It began with the patriotic verses of men like Rupert Brooke and ended with the vitriol and realism of Siegfried Sassoon and Wilfred Owen. The early writings of Brooke have been heavily criticised:

> If I should die, think only this of me:
> That there's some corner of a foreign field
> That is for ever England.

But in 1914 that was exactly how people were thinking. By the beginning of 1917, things had changed. Sassoon was now seriously critical of the way the war was being run. His poems are full of caustic, satirical comment that shocked society:

> Does it matter? – losing your legs? ...
> For people will always be kind,
> And you need not show that you mind
> When the others come in after hunting
> To gobble their muffins and eggs.

Wilfred Owen's depictions of life at the front are the voice of the ordinary man caught up in a conflict that he cannot understand:

> What passing bells for those who die as cattle?
> Only the monstrous anger of the guns.
> Only the stuttering rifles' rapid rattle
> Can patter out their hasty orisons.

Trying to make sense out of the horror of the trenches and no man's land was something all artists, whatever their genre or form, tried to do. They were lucky, they had the means and the skill to do it. For most of the soldiers of the First World War there was nothing to do but grin and bear it, to bury their heads and pray for the war to finally end.

unceremoniously hauled out of retirement. Nivelle's time had gone but, significantly, his legacy to the French army was something far worse than death in battle.

THE FRENCH ARMY MUTINIES

Nivelle's offensive had been the final straw for the demoralised French soldiers. Verdun had virtually crippled them; the Nivelle Offensive took them to breaking point.

The mutiny was not an ordered response, rather it was something that occurred and then spread. All along the French front soldiers simply laid down their arms and refused to fight. Fifty-four divisions took up the stance, and even those that did not join in marched towards the lines bleating like sheep. They were only too aware of what awaited them but were too exhausted and shell-shocked to do anything more about it than voice their disapproval in this way.

For some who went up at this perilous time, it wasn't bleating like sheep that allowed them to voice their feelings. Some of them chanted 'The Song of Despair':

> Goodbye life, goodbye love, goodbye all women.
> It is well finished, it is for always,
> This infamous war.
> It is in Caonne, on the plate,
> That one must leave his skin
> Because we are all condemned,
> We are sacrificed.

By pure chance the Germans did not know about the mutinies or realise that miles of the French front lines were left undefended. They, too, were exhausted. Nivelle's offensive had cost them over 80,000 dead or captured, and it is possible that they were content to sit and lick their wounds. For whatever reason, they did not know, which was just as well for the French. Had they realised, they could have simply walked through the French lines and been in Paris within a few days.

Petain, the new French commander, acted swiftly to stop the mutinies. Over 90,000 soldiers were court-martialled, 23,000 being found guilty. Originally 432 were sentenced to death, but clemency was now the order of the day and, eventually, no more than fifty-five of the main leaders were actually shot.

The mutinies stopped fairly quickly, and Petain guaranteed to look at issues such as extra rations and a decent leave allowance for all soldiers. Yet the situation remained delicate. Petain, and the other Allied leaders, knew that the French Army would not regain its position as an effective fighting force for many months. For some time to come the weight of continuing the war would rest on the shoulders of Douglas Haig and the British Army.

THE U-BOAT THREAT

Britain might have been imposing an effective blockade on Germany, but by 1917 the U-boats were also tightening their grip around the British coast. That April, more than a million tons of Allied and neutral shipping were sent to the bottom. Almost one vessel in four that left port bound for Britain never returned home. These were losses that were impossible to sustain, and soon American ships were refusing to sail if their destination was a British port.

The power of the submarine as a weapon of war was demonstrated in the early days of the conflict when three British cruisers – *Aboukir*, *Hogue* and *Cressy* – were torpedoed and sunk in one day. The Royal Navy also used submarines effectively, and this photograph shows the British submarine E11, commanded by Martin Nasmith, in the Dardanelles.

The answer was simple – the introduction of the convoy system. The first convoy sailed on 10 May and in the weeks ahead it was seen to be an enormous success. Sinkings dropped dramatically, and as the destroyer crews became used to working the depth charges the toll of U-boats destroyed began to rise. Soon Britain was sinking submarines faster than the German yards could build them.

In the end it was a close-run thing – at one stage there was less than a month's supply of wheat in the whole country – but by the end of the year it was clear that the convoy system was working. The U-boat threat had been nullified and in the months ahead it would be utterly destroyed.

Passchendaele (Third Ypres)

By the summer of 1917 another British assault was planned. The French still needed time to recover from the mutinies earlier in the year and the Americans had not yet begun to arrive in force. Haig was keen to finish things before the Americans began to make their presence felt. He had always favoured an attack in Flanders and now he seized the chance.

Haig's plan for the Battle of Passchendaele, or Third Ypres as it is more correctly known, was ambitious. If he could take the village and ridge of Passchendaele, he felt, there would be nothing to stop him releasing his cavalry to take the Channel ports. He did not realise that the Hindenburg Line reached up into this part of Belgium, and that key points like Pilkem Ridge were heavily defended.

The battle was one of the most horrendous ever fought. The offensive, due to begin on 23 July 1917, was postponed for seven days to allow French artillery to prepare and the opening assaults did not take place until 31 July. They continued for another three months. Canadian troops finally entered Passchendaele village on 6 November and by then the battle had cost 250,000 Allied casualties. German losses were about the same, and although Passchendaele itself had been captured it was too late in the year to allow any reasonable exploitation of the success.

The horror of Passchendaele summed up the suffering of the men in the trenches. The opening artillery barrage of the battle lasted for over a week, tons of shells raining down on the German trenches. The shelling had little effect on German defences but destroyed the drainage system of the area, breaching the canals and turning the whole front into a quagmire. To make matters worse, it began to rain on the first morning of the attack and hardly stopped for months.

The name Passchendaele is now synonymous with mud, and by the end of the first day the whole area was little more than a morass of slime. Men fell and

The Battle of Passchendaele – the Third Battle of Ypres as it is more properly known – was one of the greatest bloodbaths of the whole war. It began to rain on the first morning and rarely stopped for the next three months. Men drowned or suffocated in the shell craters and by the time the battle ground to a close in November 1917 the Allies and Germany had each lost close to 250,000 men.

drowned in the mud; they lived for weeks up to their knees in water. And the end of the war was still nowhere in sight.

THE CAPORETTO CAMPAIGN

A series of inconclusive battles between Italy and Austria-Hungary had seemed to symbolise the campaigns in the Isonzo area, with the Italians constantly attempting to drive forward into the plains beyond the mountains and the Austrians always managing to push them back. When the Italians finally managed to achieve some success in the sector in the summer of 1917, it so alarmed the Germans that Hindenburg and Ludendorff decided the Italian threat had to be eliminated once and for all.

In October a combined Austrian-German force crossed the Isonzo River and hurled itself at the Italians. The flanks of the Italian Army managed to hold but the centre, around Caporetto, quickly gave way. Reinforcements from Britain and France were rushed to the area. The Austrian-German armies were eventually fought to a standstill, but from Ludendorff's perspective it had been a successful campaign, with 200,000 Italian casualties.

THE BATTLE OF CAMBRAI

The German High Command had seen how tanks performed at the Battle of the Somme. They were not impressed and considered them to be of little value. Some limited use in the mud of Passchendaele had simply confirmed their view.

So when, on 20 November 1917, the Germans were greeted by the sight of 380 tanks trundling across the fields before them, they were more than startled. They were scared. This was the opening moment of the Battle of Cambrai. General Byng, the officer in command, had decided that there should be no preliminary bombardment. As far as he was concerned, the artillery should be saved for use

MOTOR TRANSPORT

In a war which saw the introduction of the fighter aeroplane, the development of tanks and the first concerted use of submarines, the main form of transport remained the horse. Horses pulled the guns, horses dragged ammunition lumbers, horses brought up rations and supplies.

However, as the war progressed there was a growing realisation that motor transport was the way things would go in the future. Horses needed to be fed and looked after. They could die or be seriously injured by enemy shelling. Motor transport consisted, after all, simply of pieces of metal machinery.

Gradually vans and lorries were introduced, being used to carry supplies and men, and motorbikes and armoured cars were issued to the troops. By the end of the war the more insightful observers were realising that, in the future, motorised transport was going to replace horses.

after the initial objectives had been gained – let the tanks and the element of surprise do their work.

Initially the British attack was hugely successful. Disconcerted by the tanks, the Germans abandoned their first line of trenches and fell back – the Hindenburg Line had been breached. The cavalry was immediately ordered forward, but machine-gun fire from the second and third line of trenches halted them in their tracks.

At the end of the opening day, 170 out of the 380 tanks employed that morning were out of action, either damaged by shellfire or left on the battlefield stuck in the mud. The Battle of Cambrai rumbled on for several weeks before finally ending on 5 December with 47,000 British casualties.

TANKS

Tanks – the name coming from workmen who believed they were making water tanks – were first introduced during the Battle of the Somme, where Haig had hoped they might be available for the opening attack. Despite having the cavalryman's traditional scepticism about any offensive weapon other than a horse, he was at least willing to see how these new tanks performed.

The new weapon was not ready for 1 July, however, and it was to be 15 September before the first forty-nine vehicles lumbered into action. It was not a glorious success. Nine of the tanks broke down, a dozen more were too slow to keep up with the soldiers and several more became bogged down in the mud of the battlefield. More tanks might have produced better results. As it was, there were too few of them and they were far too slow.

The psychological effect of the tanks was considerable. Initially at least, the German soldiers did not know what was coming at them. They stared in wonder and many of them ran away. Such a reaction was short-lived, as they soon saw the tanks floundering in the mud or stuck on barbed wire. Nevertheless, there was obviously potential and a little later, in November, the new weapon came into its own.

THE NOVEMBER REVOLUTION

Russia suffered a serious defeat in July 1917 and German forces even managed to reach the outskirts of Riga. Despite the best efforts of Kerensky and his provisional government, the Russians had lost all heart. The soldiers wanted simply to go home and they began to desert in droves.

Kerensky, realising that further revolution was simmering, tried to come down hard. He arrested many Bolshevik leaders and Lenin fled to Finland. When the German forces took Riga that September, General Kornilov, the Commander in Chief, realising that the war was lost, marched on Petrograd. If he could not defeat Germany, he could at least try to destroy the revolution and, perhaps, restore the Czar to his throne.

Alarmed, Kerensky armed the factory workers and released men like Trotsky from prison. He need not have bothered. Kornilov's soldiers made no attempt to capture Petrograd. They halted outside the city and either joined the Bolsheviks or simply headed off for home and safety. Trotsky and his Red Guards now had control of Petrograd and Kerensky was clinging on by his fingertips.

The cruiser *Aurora* started the second Russian Revolution and brought the Bolsheviks to power when, on the night of 25 October 1917, she fired a shot at the Winter Palace. Kerensky slipped away and Lenin and his Bolsheviks assumed control.

For several weeks nothing seemed to happen. Lenin returned from Finland, Trotsky continued to make speeches. Then, in October, Kerensky made a massive misjudgement. He closed down the Bolshevik newspaper *Pravda*, and in retaliation Trotsky seized the post office and the railway stations.

The cruiser *Aurora* was moored off the city. On the night of 25/26 October, sailors on board fired a shot at the Winter Palace, home to Kerensky's provisional government, as the signal for workers to storm the palace. Kerensky, realising his support had evaporated, left the city and slipped out of the pages of history. Lenin assumed power and immediately made peace advances.

Fighting a war on two fronts had been costly for Germany, and this was the chance to end it. An armistice was immediately signed, being converted into the Treaty of Brest-Litovsk in March the following year. Russia was out of the war.

THE DOVER PATROL

Established in 1914, the Dover Patrol was intended to provide defence for the Strait of Dover and deny the Germans access to the English Channel. The force consisted of destroyers, minesweepers, trawlers and monitors, aeroplanes and airships. At night the strait was illuminated by flares and lights on the surface as a way of preventing U-boats slipping through. The Dover Patrol, using their heavy-gunned monitors, bombarded the Belgian coast on many occasions and on St George's Day 1918 launched an assault on the submarine bases at Zeebrugge and Ostend. The attacks were costly, three obsolete cruisers filled with cement being used to block the canal and thus bottle up German U-boats in their bases, but they were successful. Eight Victoria Crosses were won during the action.

MESOPOTAMIA AND PALESTINE

Despite the disaster at Kut, by the end of 1916 the campaign in Mesopotamia was progressing satisfactorily. The plan was, after the Turks had been expelled, for Mesopotamia to become an independent state under a British mandate and thus ensure, for the foreseeable future, the oil wells of the region. Progress was slow, however, as the Turks proved a dogged and determined foe.

The lesson of Kut had been well learned. By the end of the war there were nearly 600,000 British soldiers serving in Mesopotamia, enduring the sun, sand and flies that were every bit as bad as the plagues in the Old Testament.

The original aim of the Palestine Campaign was to protect the Suez Canal. After the withdrawal from Gallipoli, the area was heavily strengthened with British and Commonwealth troops. Another Turkish attack had taken place in the summer of 1916 but it had been beaten back. In the wake of this victory it was decided that Palestine should, like Mesopotamia, also be taken from the Ottoman Empire and Britain, rather than sitting and defending the canal, went on the offensive.

At this moment a charismatic individual appeared on the scene – T. E. Lawrence or, as he is better known, Lawrence of Arabia. Much has been written about Lawrence, but the real man was practical and hard headed and knew that if the Arab nations could be brought onto Britain's side there would be far more chance of a successful outcome to the war in the Middle East. Huge sums of money were paid to the Arab leaders and they were led to believe, perhaps by Lawrence, perhaps by High Command, that once the Turks were expelled Arab independence would be guaranteed.

However, on 2 November 1917 the Balfour Declaration promised Jews from all over the world a home in Palestine. The motive was clearly financial as Jewish investors and industrialists on both sides of the Atlantic had to be kept happy.

Lawrence began a guerrilla war that saw him and his Arab helpers blow up railway tracks, buildings and bridges behind Turkish lines. He captured Aqaba and kept hundreds of Turkish soldiers engaged in defending strategic positions. Nobody knew where Lawrence and his men would appear next.

Meanwhile the Egypt Expeditionary Force prepared to move on Jerusalem. The first stage in the campaign, as everybody knew, was the capture of Gaza. Two

Lawrence of Arabia, part hero, part charlatan, part dramatic self-publicist, was one of the few men who had a direct impact on the course of the war.

attempts to take it were made in early 1917, but both resulted in failure and in 6,500 British and Commonwealth casualties.

Then the British general Archibald Murray was replaced by Sir Edmund Allenby, who had successfully commanded the Third Army at the Battle of Arras. He was an impressive man, nicknamed The Bull, and even the Anzac soldiers quickly fell under his spell.

Allenby immediately reversed previous thinking and made Beersheba the first objective, rather than Gaza. On 31 October 1917 cavalry and infantry mounted a lightning assault on Beersheba and occupied the town before the Turks knew what was happening. At the same time an assault was launched on Gaza, and Allenby's third force drove a wedge between the two towns, splitting and dividing the Turkish forces.

The key to the campaign was the Australian cavalry. Given their head, these men roamed the desert, charging the Turks wherever they found them. Towards the end of December Allenby's troops closed on Jerusalem and on the 17th of the month the city surrendered. Allenby walked calmly and respectfully into the town. This was the first time the Holy City had been in Christian hands for 600 years.

The ability of the British – soldiers and civilians alike – to laugh in the face of adversity was something that kept people going during the dark days of the war.

British Tommy (*returning to trench in which he has lately been fighting, now temporarily occupied by the enemy*). " EXCUSE ME —ANY OF YOU BLIGHTERS SEEN MY PIPE?"

Reproduced by kind permission of the Proprietors of " London " *Punch.*

HUMOUR

In the wake of bloodbaths like Passchendaele, men still managed to find things to laugh at.

Humour was there in the soldiers' songs that they sang on the march or in the estaminet, often scurrilous, often foul mouthed, but always funny. They catch the attitude of the ordinary soldier, powerless in a conflict he can do little about.

> I don't want to be a soldier,
> I don't want to go to War.
> I'd rather hang around
> Piccadilly Underground
> Living on the earnings of a high-born lady.

Sometimes there is even a degree of glee in considering what might lie ahead:

> Hush! Here comes a whiz-bang
> And it's making straight for you:
> And you'll see all the wonders of No Man's Land
> If a whiz-bang gets you.

Humorous poetry was another way of laughing at adversity. Much of it was published in *The Wipers Times*, the trench newspaper founded in February 1916. The paper's content was fertile ground for men who were willing to laugh at themselves as well as the general staff and those in command:

> Take a wilderness of ruin
> Spread with mud quite six feet deep;
> In this mud cut channels,
> Then you have the line we keep.

> Get a lot of Huns and plant them
> In a ditch across the way;
> Now you have war in the making,
> As waged here from day to day.

Humour, at least, was safe. It stopped men thinking too deeply about what faced them. Even von Hindenburg was moved to comment, 'I read no poetry now, it might soften me.' Humorous verse was different:

> There's sand and sand for miles around,
> It clogs yer mouf and eyes;
> And when yer aint a chewin' sand
> Yer chewin' bags o' flies.

> Blokes say this place aint arf so bad,
> Some say yer cannot beat it;
> I like old Egypt a bit myself
> But, blimey, not enough to eat it.

Mackain's 'Sketches of Tommy's Life' were amazingly accurate, from the puttees around the men's legs to the long service stripes on their arms. Bairnsfather's Old Bill, a character straight out of the 'Old Contemptibles', appeared many times on postcards and in booklets like 'Fragments from France'.

The British Tommy was a sentimental soul and loved nothing more than to buy and send home silk postcards that had been produced – almost as a form of cottage industry – by the women of France and Belgium. But the humorous cards of Mackain and Bairnsfather certainly ran them close, hugely popular and with enough relevance to make everyone, soldiers and their families, stop and think for a few minutes.

"The war will soon be over now."

"How's that?"

"Why Our Bill's 'listed and he's never had a job more than a fortnight."

6

1918: THE FINAL YEAR

WAR ON THE HOME FRONT

As 1918 dawned the U-boats were still not totally beaten, approximately 300,000 tons of Allied shipping being sunk every month. In February rationing of meat, sugar and butter was introduced, partly intended to curtail the activities of war profiteers. The other thing it did was to end the habit of fighting at the shop doorway for whatever food was available. Now everyone would receive a fair share.

Proving that humour was not just the preserve of the man at the front, housewives also developed the ability to laugh at deprivation, as this poem clearly shows:

> O margarine, oh margarine,
> Thy absence causes many a scene.
> I stand in queues mid snow and rain
> To get some more of Thee again.
> Fed up with jam and bloater paste,
> Oh margo, come to me in haste.

It sometimes seemed as if the war would never end. Casualty lists from France remained high and the work in the factories was more demanding than ever. More and more shells were required and while the women munitions workers were undoubtedly earning good money, there were times when they wondered if it was all worth it. The attitude of some of their male colleagues, who could not quite get it out of their minds that an effective force of women workers might just mean more unemployment after the war, was often aggressive.

The work itself was debilitating and dangerous. An explosion at a munitions factory in East London in 1917 had killed several women, and there were several more explosions, of lesser or greater degree, throughout the war as faulty

WOMEN ARE WORKING DAY & NIGHT TO WIN THE WAR

£25,000 IMMEDIATELY NEEDED FOR THE WOMEN'S WAR TIME FUND TO PROVIDE REST-ROOMS CANTEENS & HOSTELS

LORD SYDENHAM HON TREASURER

YOUNG WOMEN'S CHRISTIAN ASSOCIATION

26 GEORGE STREET HANOVER SQUARE . W

WITHERBY & Cº LONDON.

FOOD FOR THE GUNS.

Women had been employed in munitions factories since 1916, their slim hands and wrists being small enough to fit easily inside the shell casings. It was a task they carried out admirably. But as the Ludendorff Offensive gathered momentum – followed by the Allied counter-attacks – they were called on to work even harder and longer hours.

workmanship or poor materials caused serious detonations. Even if there was no explosion women would often suffer from ailments like coughs and convulsions, and the story of the 'canaries', women whose skin and hair had been turned bright yellow by the chemicals used, is now famous.

It was not just in the factories that women were now employed. The Women's Land Army and Women's Forage Corps had been established by Meriel Talbot and Lady Denman in 1917, the aim being to use women workers in traditional male farming roles in order to help food production.

PEOPLE'S SHRINES

War memorials for ordinary soldiers were almost unknown in Britain before the First World War, and those memorials that do exist for before that time tend to commemorate officers and the sons of landed gentry.

The fallen of the First World War came from a different class. Now the casualties were ordinary, decent men who had enlisted in order to help their country in time of need. They needed to be commemorated.

After 1916 makeshift shrines began to appear on village greens, on street corners and on the pavements. Not officially sanctioned, they were just an outpouring of sentiment and emotion, usually consisting of crosses, mementos and flowers. Once in place, they were added to by other bereaved relatives.

Many churches began to keep rolls of honour. These were simply lists of parishioners who had died, a compilation of sacrifice, and were given a place of honour in the church. In years to come these rolls of honour were to be the basis for each town's war memorial, but for now they were incomplete and needed to be added to every week.

THE LUDENDORFF OFFENSIVE

The German Armistice with Russia in November 1917 meant that Hindenburg and Ludendorff could now release the huge forces they had been obliged to maintain on the Eastern Front. Fifty-two divisions were quickly moved to France, ready for what would clearly be a final push for victory.

This time there was to be no prolonged preliminary bombardment to warn the enemy or destroy the ground, and the attacking troops were moved quietly up to the front at night. Importantly, unlike all previous assaults, this one was not going

The Kaiser with Field Marshal von Hindenburg.

to involve long lines of men attacking across a broad front. Units of fast-moving storm troops would rush forward to capture key points, leaving any pockets of resistance for the second or third wave of attackers to wipe out.

On 21 March 1918 Ludendorff struck. That morning the countryside was blanketed by dense fog and a short but intense bombardment in the area between Arras and St Quentin decimated the British positions. Soon the British were retreating, falling back 40 miles and sustaining 200,000 casualties.

Haig, who had always been contemptuous of the idea of supreme command, at last began to see the value of a united approach. At a meeting in Doullens on 26 March, with British forces still retreating, Ferdinand Foch was given supreme command of all Allied armies. It was an appointment that seemed to please everyone.

Foch could not direct or command the armies of the Allies as they fought. That was down to individual commanders. But he could control the reserves and he quickly showed himself adept at using such forces. Rather than throw in reserves or extra troops just to shore up a crumbling defence, he kept them back and, when the time was right, used them to counter attack.

The German attack gradually began to lose its impetus about two weeks into the campaign. On 5 April it was halted, with both sides exhausted and desperate for a respite. The Germans had inflicted heavy casualties on the enemy but they had also suffered themselves from the stubborn resistance.

Importantly, as they advanced the Germans had seen the quality and quantity of British equipment and supplies. They had come across French shops and farmhouses where there was no such thing as food shortages. As the advance began to lose its way many of the German soldiers, used to the privations imposed by the British blockade on their homeland, became more interested in plundering the wine and food than they were in attacking the enemy.

The respite was short lived. On 9 April, phase two of the Ludendorff Offensive began. This time the attack was in Flanders, on the front between Armentières and La Bassée, and was again preceded by a short but intense artillery bombardment. A 30-mile gap was smashed in the Allied line.

The fear now was that Amiens and Hazebrouck, important railway junctions, might fall. Foch quickly deployed men behind Amiens and Haig threw his last troops into the battle. It was now that he issued his famous order of the day:

> With our backs to the wall and believing in the justice of our cause each one must fight to the end – There is no other course open to us but to fight it out. Every position must be held to the last man.

German troops advanced steadily, re-taking Passchendaele. Soon even the Ypres salient and the town itself were under serious threat. Four French divisions were sent to the area between Ypres and the coast to help the Belgians defend their last piece of unoccupied territory and by 29 April the German attack had again run out of steam.

A pause of about a month now occurred as the Germans prepared for a new assault. Ludendorff knew that he could not delay for long – the longer he waited, the stronger the Allies became as American troops were now pouring into France. Unfortunately for Ludendorff, his soldiers had been ground down by pressure of their own offensives, in precisely the same way that the British and French had been worn down by their repeated offensives of the past four years.

Ludendorff's aim this time was to attack the French along the Notre Dame ridge, an area that was considered quiet and isolated. It was for this reason that Haig and Foch had sent the British IX Corps to the region. They had been severely mauled in the earlier offensives and, for the moment, Haig did not consider them in any condition to act as front-line troops. Yet that was exactly what they became when the German assaults began with what was now a usual ferocious but short-lived bombardment on 27 May.

Fourteen German divisions quickly broke through the British and French lines, advancing 10 miles in a single day, and within a week German forces had reached the River Marne, just 50 miles from Paris. French losses amounted to nearly 100,000, British to 28,000. Once again, however, German troops were disheartened by the quality of equipment they found, equipment that had been abandoned or discarded by Allied troops as they fled the battlefield.

A week later Ludendorff's troops crossed the Marne, but now the French had withdrawn to take up positions on either side of Rheims. From there they were able to shell and machine-gun the advancing Germans in what became known as the Second Battle of the Marne. It was Ludendorff's last throw of the dice. Realising the position was untenable, he pulled his forces back over the Marne and decided to go on the defensive until the Allies had been worn down.

THE ALLIED COUNTER-ATTACK

On 24 July Foch called Haig, the American general Pershing, and Petain to a meeting at his headquarters. It was time, he had decided, to go on the offensive. The British would attack in the north, around the Ypres area; the French would advance in the centre; and the Americans would assault the southern sector near the old battleground of Verdun.

On 8 August the British offensive began. They had learned something from the recent German attacks, and this time there was no prolonged bombardment before troops went over the top. In addition over 450 tanks, heavy Mark Vs and lighter, speedier Whippets, were used, and to everyone's surprise an advance of 6 miles was made before the attack slowed and stalled. Sensing the significance, Ludendorff called 8 August 'the black day of the German Army'.

Over the next few weeks Allied attacks were launched on various parts of the German lines. In the last of them, on 12 September, the Americans overran the St Mihiel salient to the south of Verdun, a success they achieved in just forty-eight hours. Pershing had insisted that the Americans should fight independently, and while earlier American assaults along the line of the Meuse had failed dismally, this time they achieved amazing success. Co-ordinated air attacks, with low-flying fighters under Colonel Billy Mitchell strafing the German troops, were an important part of the American success.

The Allied attacks were another psychological nail in the coffin of the German Army, utterly destroying the belief in German invincibility. They would continue to fight, but now no German soldier had any real hope of victory. By 18 September the British First, Third and Fourth Armies stood in front of the Hindenburg Line, positions they had held before the Ludendorff Offensive began back in March.

The Hindenburg Line was finally breached by British forces on 5 October and now the German Army, although still fighting bravely, was pushed back on all fronts. By 1 November the British had reached the Scheldt. It really did seem as if the end might be in sight.

OTHER THEATRES OF WAR

If the summer and early autumn of 1918 saw huge Allied successes in France, there were also further victories in other parts of the world.

At the end of 1917 French President Georges Clemenceau had recalled General Sarrail from Salonika, leaving Franchet d'Espèrey in command. The expeditionary force had been idle for so long that it came as something of a surprise when, on 15 September 1918, d'Espèrey decided to attack. It was a major surprise for the Bulgarians, too. Poorly equipped and demoralised, they surrendered immediately. Bulgaria asked for an armistice and promptly withdrew from the war.

Another front was opened when, on 2 August, an Allied force under General Poole landed at Archangel in Russia. The expeditionary force came courtesy of an invitation from the 'White Russians', supporters of the deposed Czar. It was an ill-fated campaign that ran on for a few years but was, inevitably, doomed to failure. Archangel was eventually abandoned and returned to Russian control. It had been a totally pointless affair, as one disgruntled British participant confirmed:

> I remember the cold, more than anything else. I was serving on board a Royal Fleet Auxiliary tanker at the time. We were just frozen in, couldn't get out or do anything. It was so cold that if you touched anything metal you'd pull your skin off when you tried to let go. I don't think we did anything useful. We just sat there.
>
> Conversation with Robert Turnbull Carradice, transcript held by author

That autumn, on the Italian Front, General Diaz launched an attack on the town of Vittorio Veneto, splitting the Austro-Hungarian Army in two. The Italians, heavily reinforced by the British Tenth Army, occupied Vittorio Veneto on 29 October and, realising they could not continue the war, the Austro-Hungarians promptly asked for an armistice. This was duly agreed and signed on 3 November.

The surrender signalled not just the end of the Austrian Army but also the end of the Austro-Hungarian Empire. In January 1918, when he had published his famous 'Fourteen Points', President Wilson had already promised that nations like Poland and Czechoslovakia should become independent states – such decisions, he declared, must lie within the remit of the countries themselves, not their previous rulers.

Within days of the armistice being signed Hungary had broken away from the old Hapsburg Empire and Czechoslovakia also announced itself an independent republic at exactly the same moment.

In the Middle East events were also rapidly moving to a climax. Allenby reached Damascus on 1 October and another Allied army was inching ever closer to the rich oilfields of Mosul. The fighting was still hard and furious but finally, facing defeat, Turkey had little alternative but to ask for terms. Turkish forces duly surrendered on 30 October, the treaty being signed on board the battleship HMS *Agamemnon*.

In East Africa the redoubtable von Lettow-Vorbeck continued to harry the British right to the end. A joint British-Portuguese force eventually forced him into Tanganyika and then into Northern Rhodesia. Faced with no alternative, von Lettow-Vorbeck surrendered, undefeated. By this time his army had been reduced to just 1,300 troops, but he had effectively kept 200,000 Allied soldiers at bay for several years, a truly significant achievement.

THE END OF THE WAR APPROACHES

As early as January 1918 American President Woodrow Wilson had put forward his 'Fourteen Points'. These were a series of suggestions that, Wilson hoped, would prevent anything like the First World War from ever occurring again. They included items like the outlawing of secret treaties, making the oceans of the world free for everyone, and self-determination for all nations. They also included the creation of a League of Nations that would arbitrate for all countries, big or small.

With defeat staring him in the face, Ludendorff now began looking for a way out. He decided that Germany needed to become a democratic nation and with amazing autocratic arrogance duly imposed this on the country. Prince Max of Baden, a liberal, was appointed chancellor and Social Democrats were even pulled into the government.

It was, of course, all a sham. Ludendorff and the other generals intended to use Prince Max and the 'Fourteen Points' merely as a way of stopping hostilities, leaving the German Army unbroken and ready to fight again at some stage in the future.

On 4 October the Germans asked for an armistice, sending their request to President Wilson, a man they considered idealistic and weak. But if Prince

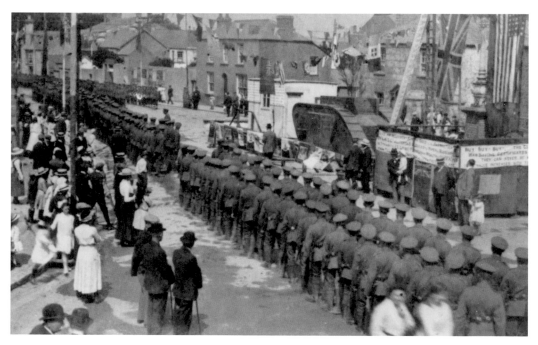

A war bonds rally to raise money to buy tanks and other military hardware.

The Armistice was signed in a railway carriage in the forest of Compiègne and hostilities ceased at 11 a.m. on 11 November 1918. There were no handshakes, both sides leaving the meeting only with regret and sorrow.

Max thought he was deluding Wilson then he was wrong. Wilson replied that any armistice had to be settled by the relevant military commanders and, most importantly, unrestricted submarine warfare must stop immediately.

When the German leaders met to discuss the situation on 17 October Ludendorff had changed his mind. The Allied offensive, he now thought, was running out of steam and there was virtue in carrying on the fight. Prince Max and the new democratic government disagreed and dismissed such a view as delusional.

Unrestricted submarine warfare was called off and Wilson's condition that an armistice had to be settled by the military leaders was accepted. And then the haggling began. Unlike the idealistic Wilson, the idea of a just peace did not appeal to any of the European leaders – they wanted their revenge and the spoils of victory.

As negotiations continued, men continued to die. The Allied armies moved steadily forward, progress being held up by stubborn German resistance. They knew that conditions in Germany were desperate, knew that the British blockade had inflicted serious food shortages on German civilians. They knew that they were winning the war but it was anybody's guess as to when the conflict might finish.

PEACE AT LAST

On 26 October, Kaiser Wilhelm unexpectedly dismissed Ludendorff and left Berlin, bound for Army Headquarters at Spa. The position was clearly desperate, and when Austria-Hungary pulled out of the war in early November it left Germany cruelly exposed.

German naval leaders now decided that it was time to pitch the High Seas Fleet, for one last time, against the might of the Royal Navy. It was to be a death-or-glory affair that could only ever end one way, and the sailors simply refused to sail. They had no desire to die at this late stage and on 29 October they mutinied. The town and port of Kiel were soon in their hands and the new democratic government in Berlin saw shades of the Russian Revolution swarming towards them. There was no alternative but to seek a peace agreement before revolution overwhelmed everything.

Matthias Erzberger, a leading Jewish politician, was appointed to head the German Armistice Commission. At 8.00 a.m. on 8 November he and other delegates met with General Foch and Admiral Wemyss in a railway carriage in the Forest of Compiègne. Foch read out the terms by which the Allies would agree to a ceasefire. They could hardly be refused. Nevertheless, Erzberger asked for time to consider and passed on the terms and conditions to Berlin.

By now the revolutionaries had taken to the streets of Berlin and a republic was proclaimed. Prince Max handed over control to Ebert, leader of the Social Democratic party, and at military headquarters the news was broken to the Kaiser. He was told that while the soldiers might well continue to fight for Germany they would no longer fight for an emperor. Kaiser Wilhelm immediately went into exile in Holland and two days later formally signed his abdication.

The new republican government quickly ordered Erzberger to sign the armistice agreement. There was no other way of avoiding revolution. The agreement was signed at 5.00 a.m. on 11 November and fighting along the Western Front ceased at 11 that morning. In the Forest of Compiègne, Foch nodded briefly to Erzberger and left the carriage without shaking hands. The war was finally over.

7

THE AFTERMATH

OCCUPATION AND DEFEAT

German troops immediately laid down their arms. Allied forces promptly moved up to the left bank of the Rhine and took control of three bridgeheads, the British at Cologne, the French at Mainz and the Americans in Coblenz. These were occupying troops, land for 50 miles beyond each bridgehead coming under Allied control.

On 21 November the German High Seas Fleet also surrendered, sailing into Scapa Flow behind the light cruiser *Cardiff*. Having obtained the fleet, nobody in the British government really knew what to do with the ships and they lay rusting at their moorings for the next seven months. But with their crews still on board, it was inevitable that something had to happen and in the summer of 1919,

> German flags rose to the mastheads of over seventy vessels – and then they began to sink. The *Frederich der Grosse*, the *Konig*, the *Von der Tann*, battleships and battle cruisers that had been the pride of the Kriegsmarine, slowly settled at their moorings and disappeared beneath the waves.

The German sailors had scuttled their ships rather than leave them in captivity, a gesture of defiance that exasperated and annoyed the British but which, really, had little overall effect.

Germany's air force had been disbanded almost immediately the Armistice was signed, the planes broken up or scrapped. It was the same with weapons like tanks, machine guns and artillery pieces. The machines of war were being taken away from Germany and there was not, as yet, even a peace treaty in place.

A total of 8,538,315 men had been killed in the conflict; another 21,219,452 had been wounded or injured. Over 5 million Britons had taken part in the war, and nearly 800,000 of them were killed. Some 12 million tons of shipping had gone to the bottom of the ocean and, in the wake of the war, Spanish flu was ravaging the world – arguably, more died from flu than were killed in the war.

Old empires had disintegrated under the pressure of war, the Hapsburg, Romanov and Ottoman dynasties simply disappearing in the latter stages of the conflict. The beginnings of new power bases, the USSR in particular, were seen for the first time and the USA confirmed itself as the most powerful nation in the world. The British Empire had bankrupted itself and was already dead in the water.

THE TREATY OF VERSAILLES

The Paris Peace Conference began its work at Versailles on 18 January 1919. The four main participants were Lloyd George of Britain, Clémenceau of France, America's President Wilson and Orlando of Italy.

There was no German or Austrian involvement at Versailles. Instead, German delegates were arbitrarily summoned on 7 May and told the terms they were now expected to sign. Failure to do so would result in a resumption of the war. Germany was exhausted, her army and navy already destroyed. She had no alternative and in the famous Hall of Mirrors her delegates signed the treaty.

The peace terms were harsh, designed to make Germany suffer and pay for the war. The mood at Versailles had been bitter, the Allied nations seeming to be greedy for revenge. Clause 231, forcing Germany to accept full blame for the conflict, was a particularly bitter pill for them to swallow. The reparations or war-damage money Germany had to pay – amounting to billions of pounds – effectively ruined her economy for years to come.

Alsace-Lorraine, seized by Germany after the Franco–Prussian War, was returned to France, while German territory and land on the west bank of the Rhine was to be occupied by Allied forces for the next fifteen years. This, Clémenceau believed, would provide a buffer between France and Germany. It also denied Germany the great industrial wealth of the Saar basin and the Ruhr coalfield.

Germany was also to lose all her colonies, which became mandates under British and French control. Her army was reduced to just 100,000 men and she was allowed no air force at all. Her navy was severely limited, her fleet having already been impounded and the number of sailors she was allowed was restricted to 15,000. She was to have no submarines of any sort.

The Treaty of Versailles was a vindictive and, ultimately, self-destructive piece of legislation that caused huge resentment in Germany and in the minds of most Germans. Five treaties were drawn up between 1919 and 1920, one for each of the defeated nations – Germany, Austria, Hungary, Bulgaria and Turkey.

Between them they changed the map of Europe and created new countries like Czechoslovakia, Estonia, Latvia and Lithuania.

Poland, an ancient kingdom that had been swallowed up by Russia and Germany many years before, was recreated and given a strip of land taken from Germany, the Polish Corridor, to allow Poles access to the sea. Hitler's quest to reclaim the Polish Corridor was, like Gavrilo Princip's shooting of Franz Ferdinand, the spark that was soon to ignite another worldwide war.

THE GREAT CLEAR-UP

In the wake of the Treaty of Versailles the killing fields of Flanders and France began to return to normal. Within a few years the trench systems were ploughed over and returned to their pre-war state, even though farmers still dig up unexploded shells every year.

It was not long before trips were being operated to the battlefields – war tourism had arrived. Many of the early visitors were people who had lost friends or relatives in the conflict – few soldiers made the return journey. They had seen enough of the battlefields to last a hundred years.

The Imperial (soon to be renamed Commonwealth) War Graves Commission began its work, cemeteries being created across northern France. The bodies of soldiers, buried out of necessity on the battlefield, were exhumed and reburied in these simple but evocative graveyards that are still visited by thousands every year.

In 1920 the body of an unidentified soldier was brought from France and buried in Westminster Abbey. The date for the ceremony was 11 November 1920. The Unknown Soldier symbolised the thousands of men who had died in the war, particularly those who had no known grave, touching the hearts of everyone.

The Cenotaph in Whitehall, designed by the architect Sir Edwin Lutyens, was never intended to be a permanent monument, the original being made out of wood and board. But the popularity of the people's shrines and the demand for permanent monuments to the fallen caused a radical change of mind. The Cenotaph, created out of Portland stone, is now the centre of the Armistice Day parade and commemoration every November.

Virtually every community in Britain demanded and got its own war memorial. It has been estimated that there are over 35,000 memorials in the country, most of them bearing Kipling's choice of words – 'Their name liveth for ever more.'

All over Britain towns and cities celebrated peace and the return of their soldiers with Victory Day parades. Sometimes these parades were delayed and did not take place until two years after the war ended. The original plans for demobilisation divided men into groups, those who had jobs to go to being discharged first. This often led to a situation where the last men in were the first men out and was clearly unfair. The government tried hard to facilitate the release of time-served men but, with Germany still occupied, demob took time. By February 1920 there were still 125,000 'hostilities only' soldiers waiting to go home.

For many, however, there could be no coming home. For many there was not even a known grave. These were men who had just disappeared, perhaps blown to pieces by shells or perhaps drowned in the mud of Passchendaele. They were commemorated on the memorials at Thiepval on the Somme and on the Menin Gate in Ypres. The two memorials remain a hugely powerful and significant statement to man's inhumanity to man. And their greatest tragedy is that they have not stopped war recurring, time after time. The belief that this, the First World War, was the war to end all wars has been proven to be an utter fallacy.

The cost of war: crosses in Flanders Fields.

WHAT NEXT?

FICTION

Barker, Pat, *Regeneration*
Carradice, Phil, *The Black Chair*
Harris, John, *A Covenant with Death*
Johns, W. E., *Biggles of the Camel Squadron*
Reeman, Douglas, *H.M.S. Saracen*
Sheriff, R. C., *Journey's End*
Yeates, Victor, *Winged Victory*

NON-FICTION

Carradice, Phil, *People's Poetry of World War One* (London: Cecil Woolf, 2008)
Press, John & Roger, *Trench Songs of the First World War* (London: Cecil Woolf, 2008)
Taylor, A. J. P., *The First World War* (London: Penguin, 1963)

POETRY

Anthologies
Gardner, Brian (ed.), *Up the Line to Death: The War Poets 1914–1918* (Methuen, 1964)
Head, Vivian (ed.), *War Poems* (Bookmart, 2009)
Noakes, Vivien (ed.), *Voices of Silence: The Alternative Book of First World War Poetry* (Sutton, 2006)

Individual Poems
Gurney, Ivor, 'First Time In'
Owen, Wilfred, 'Dulce et Decorum est', 'Inspection'
Rosenberg, Isaac, 'Break of Day in the Trenches'
Sassoon, Siegfried, 'Blighters', 'The General'
Seger, Alan, 'I Have a Rendezvous with Death'

TV

All the King's Men (1999)
Birdsong (2012)
Blackadder Goes Forth (1989)
My Boy Jack (2007)
The Wipers Times (2013)

FILMS

Aces High (1976)
All Quiet on the Western Front (1930)
Lawrence of Arabia (1962)
Oh! What a Lovely War (1969)
Private Peaceful (2012)
The Spy in Black (1939)

INDEX

Forthcoming Illustrated Introductions

Fascinated by history? Wish you knew more?
The Illustrated Introductions are here to help.

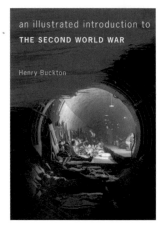

An Illustrated Introduction to the
Second World War
978-1-4456-3848-5
£9.99
Available from August 2014

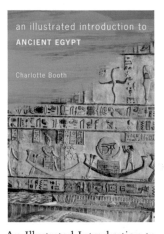

An Illustrated Introduction to
Ancient Egypt
978-1-4456-3365-7
£9.99
Available from July 2014

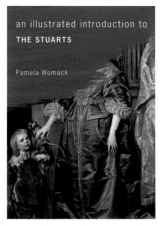

An Illustrated Introduction to the Stuarts
978-1-4456-3788-4
£9.99
Available from September 2014

Available from all good bookshops or to order direct
Please call **01453–847–800**
www.amberleybooks.com